GLOBETROTTER™

Trav

CW00376768

ZANZIBAR

GRAHAM MERCER

NEW
HOLLAND

NEW
HOLLAND

★★★ Highly recommended
★★ Recommended
★ See if you can

First edition published in 2009
by New Holland Publishers (UK) Ltd
London • Cape Town • Sydney • Auckland
10 9 8 7 6 5 4 3 2 1
website: www.newhollandpublishers.com

Garfield House, 86 Edgware Road, London W2 2EA,
United Kingdom

80 McKenzie Street, Cape Town 8001, South Africa

Unit 1, 66 Gibbes Street, Chatswood NSW 2067,
Australia

218 Lake Road, Northcote, Auckland, New Zealand

Distributed in the USA by
The Globe Pequot Press, Connecticut

This guidebook has been written by independent authors
and updaters. The information therein represents their impar-
tial opinion, and neither they nor the publishers accept pay-
ment in return for including in the book or writing more
favourable reviews of any of the establishments. Whilst every
effort has been made to ensure that this guidebook is as
accurate and up to date as possible, please be aware that the
facts quoted are subject to change, particularly the price of
food, transport and accommodation. The Publisher accepts
no responsibility or liability for any loss, injury or inconvenience incurred by readers or travellers using this guide.

Publishing Manager: Thea Grobbelaar
DTP Cartographic Manager: Genené Hart
Editor: Carla Zietsman
Design and DTP: Genené Hart
Cartographer: Inga Ndibongo
Picture Researcher: Felicia Apollis
Consultant: Melissa Shales
Proofreader: Thea Grobbelaar
Reproduction by Resolution (Cape Town).
Printed and bound by Times Offset (M) Sdn. Bhd.,
Malaysia.

Keep us Current
Information in travel guides is apt to change, which is why
we regularly update our guides. We'd be grateful to receive
feedback if you've noted something we should include in
our updates. If you have new information, please share it
with us by writing to the Publishing Manager, Globetrotter,
at the office nearest to you (addresses on this page). The
most significant contribution to each new edition will
receive a free copy of the updated guide.

Acknowledgments:
The author would like to acknowledge the help and
encouragement he received from: Elizabeth and Seif M
Miskry (Flame Tree Hotel, Nungwi); Georges E Noel
(Sunrise Hotel, Bwejuu); the owners, management and
staff of the Sau Inn, Jambiani; Raf Jah (Kervan Saray
Lodge, northwest Pemba); Anwar Beiser (Blue Oyster
Hotel, Jambiani); Kaare Johansen (Manta Reef Lodge,
northwest Pemba); Christian Moorhouse Chilcott (Scuba-
Do Diving, Zanzibar); Luca Crudelli; Abdul Aziz (Tembo
Hotel, Stone Town); and the owners, management and
staff of the Mbweni Ruins Hotel just south of Stone Town,
as well as many other people in Zanzibar, too numerous
to mention in full. Among the latter is that outstanding
teacher and raconteuse, Patricia Barrett, who taught and
lived in Zanzibar for several years and has always loved
it; that other outstanding teacher and lover of Zanzibar
Gloria Mawji; and Navneet and Raksha Shah, Bridget
Morgan, Jamila (of the International School of Zanzibar),
Sati Ghadvi and her delightful twin daughters Arzoo and
Anmol, Kevin Bartlett and last but not least the author's
wife Anjum, to whom this book is dedicated. Thanks also
to the administration, Board and staff of the International
School of Tanganyika (IST) in Dar es Salaam, without
whose generosity and support the author and his wife
could not have stayed on in Tanzania.

Photographic Credits:
Peter Blackwell/Images of Africa: pages 4, 6, 11, 12, 18,
21, 24, 28, 31, 34, 35, 37, 41, 60, 64, 70, 75, 102, 119;
Luca Crudelli: pages 100, 106, 108, 110, 113, 116;
Roger de la Harpe/Africa Imagery: pages 86, 94;
Elinore de Lisle: pages 74, 84;
Corrie Hansen/Images of Africa: page 22;
Graham Mercer: pages 7, 14, 32;
Ian Michler/Images of Africa: pages 19, 56, 63, 66, 76,
80, 97;
Peter Ribton/Images of Africa: pages 39, 42, 45;
Duncan Smith: cover, pages 15, 17;
Ariadne van Zandbergen/Images of Africa: title page,
pages 26, 48, 52, 79;
Andrew Woodburn/Images of Africa: pages 111, 120

Cover: *The House of Wonders in Stone Town.*
Title Page: *Dhows passing Zanzibar waterfront.*

CONTENTS

1
Introducing Zanzibar

Zanzibar captured the heart of an Omani sultan in 1828, and the imagination of the rest of us (including many honeymooners) ever since. Its name reeks of 'tropic isles' romanticism as the islands, just off the coast of Tanzania, East Africa, still sometimes reek of cloves. In the 19th century, however, Unguja (Zanzibar Island) reeked less fragrantly; David Livingstone called it 'Stinkibar', and even today tourists sometimes have to side-step the odd dead rat or, in the rains, a stream of 'light sewage', as they stroll through the bazaars of Stone Town, Unguja's historic capital. Not what tourists think of as they daydream of exotic isles, though 'exotic' merely means 'alien', 'introduced from abroad', 'outlandish' or even 'barbarous'; Zanzibar's history covers the lot. But if we wanted sanitized streets and a spotless past we could go elsewhere, and in doing so miss a fascinating experience, for despite its faults (or because of them), Zanzibar is as beguiling as its reputation.

It is not one island but an archipelago, consisting of Unguja, Pemba and a host of smaller islands. None are topographically dramatic, but what they lack in grandeur they make up for in Eastern charisma and mystique, historic importance and (in their western regions) the richness of their soil, so fertile that Zanzibaris claim they can plant a walking stick and it will sprout leaves; hence the profusion of aromatic crops that gives Zanzibar its 'Isles of Spices' epithet, and a similar profusion of fruits, their names alone enough to make the mouth water.

TOP ATTRACTIONS

***Stone Town:** lose yourself in the bazaars and narrow streets.
***Take a **boat trip** to the offshore islands of **Changuu, Bawe** and **Chumbe** for snorkelling.
***Diving/snorkelling off **Mnemba Island**, Unguja.
***A **Spice Tour**.
***A boat trip to **Misali Island**, Pemba.
***Diving/fishing/snorkelling** at the various sites around the islands.
***Wonderful **beaches** and **resorts**, especially at Kendwa, Nungwi and along the east coast of Unguja.

Opposite: *A Swahili girl in Stone Town.*

**THRUST INTO
THE LIMELIGHT**

According to geologists the
Zanzibar archipelago is composed of rocks ranging in age
from the Miocene epoch to
geologically recent limestone
sediments covered, over the
ages, by silts and clays
washed down by mainland
rivers. Much of the archipelago was probably once
covered by the sea, the
islands that we see today
thrust above the surface by
the phenomenon known as
block-faulting.

Not all the land is bountiful. Much of the south and
east of Unguja is as hard and uncompromising as the
coral rag that underlies it, but as if to make up for this
apparent lapse, nature has graced the island's eastern
coast with broad swathes of sand, so fine-grained and
white you half-expect it to dissolve when the tide
comes in, like coffee creamer. These beaches, backed
by palms and casuarinas, slope into seas of every shade
of blue, as if fleets of treasure ships, loaded with aqua-
marine, sapphires, turquoise and lapis lazuli, had
foundered in some ancient storm and scattered their
cargoes over the ocean floor. There are beautiful
beaches elsewhere also, and along Pemba's much-
indented shores coves so secluded that many are accessible only by sea.

It is the ocean that draws most tourists to Zanzibar,
not only to swim, sail or snorkel in its shallows but to
explore its depths; the coral gardens that coruscate with
brilliant fish, anemones and nudibranches; the plunging
walls of the outer reefs where giants of the deep glide
by in submarine sublimity; or the open seas, where
game-fishing boats pit their wits against a host of feisty
fighting fish.

But it is Zanzibar's history that makes it unique.
Sometimes bloody, always international and fascinat-
ing, the islands' past is concentrated in Unguja's **Stone
Town** and along its famous waterfront, across the har-

Below: *Secluded sands
and exposed coral at
Matemwe, on Zanzibar's
northeast coast.*

bour of which lie ghost
dhows that are, in basic
form, historic in them-
selves. In the narrow
streets beyond, the imag-
inative traveller, dreamily
lost in thought and in the
intricate maze of lanes
and alleys, half-expects to
turn a corner and bump
into a celebrated 19th-
century explorer, a sub-
dued file of slaves on

their way to market or a sultan's lavish procession. The hole-in-the-wall *dukas* in the bazaars are now more likely to sell souvenirs than sacks of rice, but structurally they too are unchanged. The coral blocks of the Arab houses, the carved and studded teak of iconic Zanzibar doors, the fretworked balconies and shutters of Gujarati-style upper storeys, all these ooze history as the spice shops ooze fragrance.

In the bazaars you can rub shoulders with the people who make Zanzibar so exhilarating: the modest Muslim girls in their deceptively simple *buibui* and *hijab*, the men in casual western clothes or ankle-length white *kanzu* and Muslim *kofia*, the mainland Africans now living in Unguja or over on business, and an international directory of travellers and tourists. And of course the flotsam and jetsam that all societies produce: the drug addicts, touts and beggars, though even these, in easy-going Zanzibar, rarely persist if their entreaties are politely but firmly declined.

Zanzibar, after all, is not quite paradise on earth; it has known the abominations of war and slavery, savage revolution, depravity and depression, and political dissatisfaction persists, as do the abuses of power such as corruption and nepotism, but these negatives serve to accentuate the positives, as the shadows of Stone Town accentuate the light. Zanzibar could undoubtedly be a better place, though hardly a more interesting one. Said the Great, the sultan who fell in love with Zanzibar so long ago, would have known this; he was no innocent. He loved Zanzibar, as you must learn to do, for all its faults, as well as for its multitudinous pleasures.

Above: *A woman walks with a Zanzibari slowness through Stone Town's narrow lanes.*

PERFUMED GARDEN

Few perfumes have the mystique associated with Arabian *oud*. Made from the fragrant resin of *Aquilaria* trees, *oud* is the aloe mentioned in the Bible, valued for thousands of years as an aphrodisiac or (for those more seriously inclined) as an aid to spiritual meditation. In Zanzibar it is often burned in a small clay bowl, in the fumes of which a woman might steep her clothes or presumably (we are in the realms of fantasy here) her naked body.

THE LAND

Zanzibar consists of Unguja and Pemba and 50 or so smaller islands, separated from the northern Tanzanian coast by the Zanzibar and Pemba channels respectively. The latter, some 65km (40 miles) wide, is in places 25km (15.5 miles) broader than its Zanzibar counterpart and 20 times deeper, with a precipitous fall of up to 800m (2625ft) between it and the continental shelf. Unguja is 85km (53 miles) long and 25km (15.5 miles) wide 'across the waist', tapering prominently to the extreme north, more gently to the south. Pemba, 50km (31 miles) to the north-northeast, is roughly similar in proportion but smaller by about a quarter, and more ragged at the edges.

Pemba, much older than Unguja, was thrust from the sea by simple block-faulting and is geologically detached from the continental shelf, whereas Unguja was probably still part of the mainland at the beginning of the Pleistocene epoch. Which explains why the Zanzibar Channel varies only from 20–60m (66–197ft) in depth. Unguja's coastline is also less indented than that of Pemba, with far fewer mangrove thickets.

Zanzibar's Low Profile

Pemba is a north-south ridge corrugated by a series of erosion gullies, giving it a hilly appearance, though its highest point (Siniongoni) is less than 100m (328ft) above sea level. The island has a raised east coast and, especially in the west, a much-indented coastline, low-lying and with dense mangrove thickets.

Unguja has several broad ridges, in its case in the west and northwest, and although its highest point (Masingini) is a little higher (about 120m/394ft above sea level) than that of Pemba, the island as a whole is much flatter, with almost two-thirds of its southern and eastern regions low-lying. A few streams drain from the ridges to the sea in predominantly northerly or westerly directions but streams in the east disappear into the porous coral rag, which covers most of that side of Unguja.

Cultivation

Thanks to its higher rainfall Pemba is generally more fertile than Unguja, with 74% of the island under cultivation, compared with 46% on its larger neighbour. This is why Pemba was known to the Arabs as *Jaziirat ul Khadhraa*, the Green Island, and why it is the true Isle of Cloves, for 70% of Zanzibar's clove trees grow there. Rice is grown in isolated paddies, mostly located along the northern and eastern hinterland.

If Pemba is the true Isle of Cloves, Unguja is the Isle of Coconuts, with extensive plantations along its coasts and elsewhere, though cloves are still grown in the fertile northwest. It is here, also, that the other spices for which Zanzibar is famous are grown. Additional crops throughout the isles include millet, maize, sesame, rice, cassava, cowpeas, pigeon peas, sweet potatoes, cashew nuts and sugar cane.

By and Beneath the Ocean

Unguja's topographical 'split personality' is reflected along its coasts, with many stretches of mangroves but comparatively few beaches and coral reefs in the west and extensive mangrove-free beaches, coralline shelves and reefs in the east. Beaches in western Unguja, and throughout Pemba, tend to be relatively small. The sea still teems with fish and many other sea creatures, its bed in many places a bewitching coral wonderland, providing fishermen with a living and tourists with pleasure and adventure.

NEITHER HERE NOR THERE

There are nine species of mangrove in Zanzibar, each using various evolutionary tactics to survive in their inter-tidal zone, enduring dehydrating heat, choking mud and salinity that would kill other plants within hours. They have inbuilt filter systems to keep out most of the salt, and specially adapted roots. The black mangrove, for example, has pneumatophores (snorkel-like roots) that project above the mud, while the red has high-arching prop roots to anchor it firmly in the tidal sludge.

Land Animals

There are about 54 species of mammals (23 of them bats) in Zanzibar, mostly on Unguja. They include monkeys, bushbabies, antelopes, bushpigs, civets, squirrels and mongooses, some endemic. Sadly, the island's largest carnivore, the Zanzibar leopard, is almost certainly extinct. Smaller creatures such as frogs, lizards, spiders and insects occur in their usual tropical abundance, and at least 217 species of birds have been recorded in the archipelago.

Natural and Exotic Vegetation

The forests that once covered much of Zanzibar fall roughly into three types: moist forest (that once predominated on the deeper soils of Pemba and Unguja's western regions), dry coral rag forest (found mostly in eastern Unguja) and mangroves. The moist forest was mostly destroyed to make way for clove plantations and the coral rag thicket has suffered from shifting cultivation, firewood collection, charcoal burning and uncontrolled settlement. Mangroves have been exploited for centuries for their termite-resistant poles (*boriti*), much used in building construction.

The most significant patch (1440ha/3558 acres) of moist forest remaining in Pemba is Ngezi, its counterpart on Unguja being Jozani (2500ha/6178 acres), usually classified as ground water forest because of its high water table. Both contain exotic as well as indigenous trees, as do the islands' towns and suburbs, where many non-native species were planted for shade or decoration. Pemba has other interesting remnants of forest and woodland here and there, whilst the coral rag of eastern Unguja still supports large extents of semi-deciduous/evergreen thicket, with scatterings of larger trees, including baobabs.

Conservation

Conservation hasn't had a good track record in Zanzibar. Forests have been destroyed, reefs damaged, inshore waters (particularly the Zanzibar Channel) over-fished and wildlife badly neglected. Many abuses, such as deforestation, over-fishing, the illegal use of small-mesh nets, as well as habitat destruction (to which the plethora of new resorts has contributed), still go on, but there is an increasing awareness of the problems, and the growth in tourism, whilst exacerbating certain concerns (e.g. the harassment of dolphins at Kizimkazi), is helping to redress others. The more tourists visit Ngezi or Jozani forests, the Zanzibar Butterfly Centre at Pete, the various dive sites and reefs and places like the natural turtle aquarium at Nungwi, the more the government and people of Zanzibar might appreciate the value of such resources and the need to conserve them. And the more money they will have (assuming it is not squandered or pilfered) to spend on conservation.

Above: *A Zanzibar red colobus monkey in Jozani Forest.*

Climate

Zanzibar's climate, whilst trying at times, is generally quite pleasant. The northeast monsoon (*kaskazi*) often heralds hot, humid weather (mid-November to mid-March) but the southeast monsoon (*kusi*) brings much drier, cooler weather (mid-June to mid-October).

With the northeast monsoon come the short rains (*vuli*), normally in November, though they can extend into December. As the northeaster dies away the long rains (*masika*) begin, bringing sometimes heavy but rarely long-lasting downpours, predominantly in April and May. Pemba experiences higher rainfall than Unguja, with an average annual rate of 2083mm (82 in) compared to 1575mm (62 in). Rainfall on both is generally greater in the west.

Minimum-maximum average temperatures hover around 24/28°C (75/82°F) from December to April (inclusive) and 22/25°C (72/77°F) from July to October (inclusive).

WINDS OF CHANGE

Monsoons are basically triggered by the earth's tilt in relation to the sun. Land heats more rapidly than water, the air over the oceans therefore remaining relatively cooler. During the northern summer the sun's rays shine more directly on the northern hemisphere. Landmasses such as Africa and Asia absorb the heat and the air above them rises, causing cooler maritime air to rush in from the southern hemisphere to replace it. In the northern winter this process is reversed.

ZANZIBAR	J	F	M	A	M	J	J	A	S	O	N	D
AVERAGE TEMP °F	81	81	81	79	79	77	75	75	77	77	79	81
AVERAGE TEMP °C	27	27	27	26	26	25	24	24	25	25	26	27
RAINFALL in	3	3	5	15	10	2	2	2	2	3	9	6
RAINFALL mm	76	76	127	381	254	51	51	51	51	76	228	152
DAYS OF RAINFALL	7	6	12	19	14	4	5	6	6	7	14	12

Below: *Graves at Zanzibar's first mosque, the 12th-century house of worship at Kizimkazi.*

HISTORY IN BRIEF
Zamani Sana – A Very Long Time Ago
Zanzibar's earliest settlers were probably Bantu fishermen or farmers from the mainland, known to some historians as **Hadimu**. Those who settled in Pemba or on Tumbatu Island took on the names of their adopted homes (*Wapemba* and *Watumbatu*).

The first recorded non-African visitors were apparently the Sumerians, followed, perhaps as long ago as 2750BC, by the Assyrians, and some 2000 years later by the Persians. Arabs (including Egyptians), Indians, Phoenicians and Jews were probably familiar with the islands at least 3000 years ago.

The area was presumably known to the Ancient Greeks, for a Greek pilot, based in Egypt at about the time of Alexander the Great, wrote a seafarer's manual, *Periplus of the Erythraen Sea*, about Azania (the East African seaboard) and its trading potential; it mentions exports of ivory, tortoiseshell and rhinoceros horn in return for hatchets, daggers, glass vessels, wheat, ghee and cloth from Egypt, India and Arabia, and describes the locals as 'men of piratical habits, very great in stature' (though easily won over by a propitious bottle of wine).

The natives didn't improve with time, according to the 10th-century AD Arabian adventurer al-Masudi, who revealed that the men of Zinj (another name for the East African coast) had hanging lips and teeth sharpened with files to better enable them to gnaw on human flesh. Four centuries later Marco Polo assures us that the women of Zanzibar were 'very devils' with 'breasts…four times bigger than any other women; a very disgusting sight.' Zanzibari women must have undergone a remarkably successful slimming course since then or Marco Polo's imagination was four times bigger than anyone else's (he never set foot in Zanzibar, though he referred to it as a 'great and noble island').

Tales of cannibals and top-heavy Zanzibari women did not deter the traders, some from as far afield as China and Java (as early as the 8th century), with others from the Maldives (in the 14th). Arabs and Shirazi Persians perhaps began to settle on the islands in about AD700, though who came first and when is unclear. Certainly, Shirazis had settled at Kizimkazi, in southern Unguja, by AD1107, and Shirazis probably gave Zanzibar its name, *Zangh-i-bar*, though this is also debated.

The Shirazi/Swahili Civilizations

Arab and Shirazi settlers took African women as partners and eventually their cultures blended into one. Today, Persian and Arab bloodlines are virtually indistinguishable, though many people in Zanzibar still insist that they are Shirazi. This emergent society, today known as the Swahili Civilization, inspired the spread of Islam along the entire East African coast, and a surge in trade throughout the western Indian Ocean and the Gulf.

HISTORICAL CALENDAR

AD700 (approx.) Arabs begin to settle in the islands.
AD800 (approx.) Persians begin to settle in Zanzibar.
AD1107 Islam becomes predominant religion.
1503 Portuguese annex Unguja and Pemba.
1729 Portuguese, under pressure from Omani Arabs, leave Zanzibar.
1804 Zanzibar becomes busiest slave clearing depot along East African coast.
1822 Sultan Said signs treaty banning sale of slaves to Christians and allowing presence of British agent.
1847 Treaty banning slave trading throughout Oman's East African empire signed.
1855 Sultan Said dies.
1860s Around 21,000 slaves a year brought to Zanzibar.
1869 Cholera outbreak kills 50,000, one sixth of the population, in Zanzibar.
1872 Hurricane kills thousands and causes immense

damage in Zanzibar Town.
1873 Slave market closed forever, though some slavery continues.
1874 Livingstone's body brought back to Zanzibar.
1884 Beginning of 'Scramble for Africa'.
1886 What are now Kenya and Tanzania become British and German colonies respectively.
1888 Sultan Barghash dies.
1896 Shortest war in history (45 minutes).
1897 Sultan Hamud signs decree abolishing legal status of slavery.
1907 Slavery abolished completely in Zanzibar.
1914 World War I begins.
December 1963 Zanzibar gains independence.
1964 Bloody revolution takes place in Zanzibar and Omani sultanate overthrown. Governments of Tanganyika and Zanzibar merge to form United Republic of Tanzania,

with Julius Nyerere as president and Abeid Karume of Zanzibar vice-president.
1972 Abeid Karume assassinated in Stone Town. Aboud Jumbe takes over as president of Zanzibar.
1995 Tanzania's first multi-party elections held. Salmin Amour narrowly and controversially elected president of Zanzibar.
2000 Zanzibar again experiences bitterly disputed elections. Amani Karume emerges as president of Zanzibar.
2005 Elections in Zanzibar again marred by violent protests. Amani Karume re-elected. Zanzibar remains predominantly peaceful and tourism continues to expand.
2009 Despite global economic depression, Unguja remains popular with tourists. Pemba slowly emerges as a tourist resort, with emphasis on its superb diving opportunities.

MERCHANT PRINCE
WHO LIVED IN
A FACTORY

Sultan Said could be ruthless but was more mercantile than military. After establishing himself in Zanzibar he reduced taxes and steadily improved external trade, especially with America and Europe. As well as vastly increasing Zanzibar's clove output, he introduced Far Eastern fruits such as the durian, jackfruit and rambutan and is even said to have sold brandy to Muslim traders. He could also be disarmingly gracious and generous. The German missionary/explorer Ludwig Krapf, a Christian, paid tribute to Said's 'condescension and courtesy' in 1844, though the sultan's palace reminded him of 'a German factory'.

Below: *Seyyid Said bin Sultan.*

The Portuguese Period

The beginning of the end for this enterprising mercantile society came in 1498 with the arrival of the Portuguese, who quickly subdued the Swahili towns. In Zanzibar they launched piratical raids upon trading dhows, angering Unguja's ruler, who in 1503 mobilized a fleet of canoes, carrying 4000 men, to confront the marauders. The canoes were converted into colanders by state-of-the-art cannon and Unguja and Pemba were annexed. There was some defiance, first in Unguja and a century later in Pemba, but compared with Portuguese retribution elsewhere, Zanzibar escaped lightly and gradually settled into a more peaceful co-existence with the Europeans.

Omani forces had attacked Portuguese settlements in Zanzibar as early as 1652, killing their Roman Catholic vicar and destroying his church, but it was not until 18 months later that the Portuguese were expelled from Zanzibar forever and in 1729 fled Mombasa for Mozambique. They left behind ruined forts, rusting cannon and resentment, and a more positive heritage of cassava, groundnuts, sweet potatoes, guava, pineapples and paw-paws.

The Zanzibari Sultanate

Despite the Omani take-over, and the fact that the Omani Mazrui clan eventually made Mombasa the most powerful town in East Africa and occupied half of Pemba (1780), the Arabs were disunited and overseas trade in the region stagnated. It took a most unusual man to revive it and to lift Zanzibar from recession and relative obscurity to riches and worldwide fame, though the riches largely depended upon the sweat of slaves.

Seyyid Said bin Sultan was a decisive, determined man who in

his youth had taken a short cut (literally and figuratively) to the Omani throne by sticking a dagger into his cousin's stomach. But at heart he was an entrepreneur, known as the Merchant Prince, as well as Said the Great, and he quickly appreciated Zanzibar's potential as political base and trading centre.

Between 1832, when he transferred the seat of his sultanate from Muscat to Zanzibar, and 1856 when he died, he transformed the islands, with an economic policy founded on cloves, copra, slaves and ivory. Cloves had been introduced from the Moluccas decades earlier but Said greatly expanded their cultivation, leading from the front by planting cloves on 45 of his estates. Landowners were ordered to replace every coconut palm that fell, or was cut down, with three clove trees, or run the risk of having their lands confiscated.

Above: *The Slave Market Memorial.*

The East African Slave Trade

Said and many of his subjects relied heavily upon slavery, but they were not alone. Slavery goes back to classical times and beyond and most countries in the world, including those in Africa, were once involved in slavery or benefitted from it. The Zanzibar sultans were no exception, and from 1777 to 1876, when sultans were at their most influential in Zanzibar, more than a million human beings were sold in Unguja's slave market.

The horrors of the slave trade are indefensible. David Livingstone described the Ujiji slavers as 'the vilest of the vile' and even Richard Burton, who was at home among Arabs and not known for sentimentality, denounced slave trafficking as something that 'practically annihilates every better feeling of human nature'. The long journeys to the coast, when slaves might die of disease, be badly beaten or even murdered with impunity, must have been traumatic for them. Sea passages were even worse. Dhows were often packed with as many as 600 slaves, crammed into tiers only

DISMAL DIASPORA

After arrival in Zanzibar and after the humiliations of the slave market, about half the slaves from the mainland remained in Zanzibar, with almost a third shipped on, under appalling conditions, to Arabia, Persia or India. A little over 18% went to southeast Africa. By 1804 Zanzibar was the main clearing-house and six years later Captain Smee of the British Navy estimated that three-quarters of Zanzibar's population of 200,000 were slaves. The slavers were mostly Unguja-based Arabs or Swahili who controlled the trade routes, which penetrated deep into the interior ('When the flute is played in Zanzibar, they dance at the Lakes').

SKELETONS – BUT NOT IN THE CUPBOARDS

The custom of burying slaves alive in the walls of houses under construction is thought to have been fairly common in old Zanzibar. Skeletons were discovered in the foundations of the old Cable and Wireless building, erected on the site of the original slave market at Shangani by Sultan Barghash to bring enlightenment to Zanzibar. A more awful irony distinguishes a building called *Mambo Msiigi* (see page 35) on the tip of the Shangani promontory. It was formerly occupied by such anti-slavery luminaries as the Universities Mission to Central Africa and Sir John Kirk, who were all blithely unaware that living slaves had been entombed in the walls which sheltered them.

1m (3ft) or so apart. The British Consul Christopher Rigby wrote that slaves arriving in Zanzibar were 'frequently in the last stages of lingering starvation and unable to stand. Some drop dead in the custom house and streets. Others who are not likely to recover are left on board to die in order that the owner may avoid paying duty'.

In the interest of balance, Rigby also said (of slaves in Zanzibar, who were usually given their own plots and two days off per week to tend to them) that they led 'an easy life'. The Scottish explorer Joseph Thomson agreed, declaring that the typical slave in Unguja occupied 'a particularly comfortable position', and even Livingstone sometimes travelled with slave traders. 'The slavers', he said after one such journey, 'showed the greatest kindness and anxiety for my safety and success'. None of this excuses the slavers or condones slavery, but it suggests that life in general for slaves, once established in their working roles, especially in domestic service, was not the succession of beatings and whippings that is sometimes imagined.

Even at best, however, slavery was unacceptable. In Zanzibar British administrators such as Hamerton and Kirk exerted pressure on successive sultans. Said reluctantly signed one treaty in 1822, a second in 1845. After his death in 1856, when the succession was disputed, the British tightened their grip on Zanzibar. One of Said's sons, Thuwain, now ruled in Oman, his brother Majid in Zanzibar. Majid, founder of Dar es Salaam, died in 1870 and was replaced by his more robust, less biddable brother, Barghash.

Sultan Barghash

Barghash ruled for 18 years, a period paralleled by the British vice-consul (later consul) to Zanzibar, Scotsman John Kirk. Kirk and Barghash became good friends, though the relationship was strained to its limits in 1873 when Sir Bartle Frere arrived to present the sultan with an anti-slavery ultimatum, which Barghash rejected. Frere left Zanzibar frustrated, though he had a naval

Opposite: *Sultan Barghash ruled in Zanzibar for 18 years.*

blockade imposed on the mainland's slaving ports, reducing the number of slaves reaching Zanzibar that season to 21, compared with the usual 4000. On 3 June 1873 John Kirk confronted Barghash with the disputed 'agreement'. 'I have not come to discuss', he said, 'but to dictate.'

Barghash signed two days later and the infamous Zanzibar slave market was closed, though 25 years passed before slaves in the islands could claim their freedom. Legalized slavery went on in Zanzibar until 1911. The last slave dhow bound for the Gulf was apprehended as late as 1899 and the last slave caravan on the mainland in 1922.

The Explorers

From the mid-1840s, when the German missionary-explorers Krapf and Rebmann (first recorded outsider to see Kilimanjaro) passed through Zanzibar, a series of remarkable if not always likeable men began to leave Unguja for the mainland and the interior. These explorers followed the old trade routes to the lakes and beyond, mostly in large caravans and on foot, in often gruelling and sometimes perilous circumstances.

The earlier ones sought the source of the Nile and the fame that would come with its discovery; some found an early grave instead. In 1857 the disturbingly brilliant Richard Burton and his staid partner John Speke arrived in Unguja. Their expedition was doomed to partial failure (they were barely on speaking terms for much of the time) but Speke returned in 1859 with a less contentious companion, James Grant, and discovered the Nile's outflow from Lake Victoria.

His conclusions were debated and in 1866 the Scottish missionary-explorer David Livingstone was in Zanzibar planning his own expedition. He eventually made his base in Ujiji, by Lake Tanganyika, where all verifiable contact with the outside world was lost.

> **BRITAIN'S MAN IN ZANZIBAR**
>
> John Kirk was, perhaps, the best-known of several very able British consuls attached to Zanzibar. A former travelling partner of Livingstone's and a friend and advisor of Sultan Barghash, his influence was enormous. He helped to end the slave trade, and also assisted various explorers (although Stanley detested him). His house at Mbweni (see page 54), just south of Zanzibar Town, and built for him by Barghash, still stands (just about). It was here that Kirk, an expert botanist, lovingly created an experimental garden, introducing improved varieties of native food-plants and trees, and other plants likely to prove of economical value to the islands.

Right: '*Livingstone's House*' *in Stone Town, Zanzibar, is now the headquarters of the Zanzibar Tourist Corporation.*

SWEATSHOP TO CELEBRITY

At the age of 10, David Livingstone was sent to work in a Scottish cotton mill where he laboured from 06:00 until 20:00, after which he attended evening classes. By dour determination and hard work he qualified as a doctor and was accepted by the London Missionary Society to serve in South Africa. By the time he first arrived in Zanzibar (1866) he was already famous for his explorations in the south (including the 'discovery' of the Victoria Falls). Sultan Majid had made a house (now a tourist attraction) available to him just north of Stone Town, but the next seven years were spent deep in the African interior. Here, much of his energy was sapped in a campaign against slavery and a futile search for the source of the Nile, leading to his death in what is now northern Zambia in 1873. His body was carried to the coast by his followers and eventually buried in Westminster Abbey, London. Many Africans knew him as 'The Good One'.

Henry Morton Stanley, a little-known journalist with an astonishing past (and future), was dispatched to find him, which he famously did.

Stanley was in and out of Zanzibar in subsequent years, going on to cross Africa three times, under often excruciating circumstances. Other explorers to pass through include Joseph Thomson (first known 'outsider' to cross Maasailand) and the unassuming Verney Lovett Cameron, once compared with Livingstone, now practically forgotten.

Rule Brittania

After the closing of the slave market in 1873 the British virtually ruled Zanzibar, though Sultan Barghash (dismissed by Consul Rigby as 'a sullen, morose, discontented character' who 'detests all Europeans') achieved much. He had spring water piped into Stone Town for the convenience of its citizens and after the opening of the Suez Canal in 1869 helped to improve communications with the Western world by steamship and cable. He was accused of ostentatious living and he certainly had his palaces and harems but like his father he could be generous and fair-minded. He wasn't always lucky, either. Two serious outbreaks of cholera (the second in 1869) were followed in 1872 by a hurricane that caused thousands of deaths and much damage, not least among Unguja's clove plantations.

And by 1884 the 'Scramble for Africa' was hotting up. That November four Germans arrived in Zanzibar surreptitiously. Their leader, Carl Peters, was soon to become notorious for his Machiavellian attitudes and brutality. They slipped away to the mainland, returning the following month after 'persuading' 12 chiefs to relinquish 6477km^2 (2500 sq miles) of Africa. Barghash was incensed. 'These territories', he raged, 'are under our authority from the time of our fathers!'

Further landgrabs occurred and in August 1885 five German warships steamed into Zanzibar harbour, threatening to shell the town unless Barghash accepted the German treaties. He acquiesced. Soon Britain and Germany had carved out colonies (now Kenya and Tanzania), leaving Barghash with his islands and the mainland coastal strip. Barghash, feeling betrayed, despite the loyalty of his British friends John Kirk and General Lloyd Matthews (commander of the sultan's armed forces), became seriously ill and died in 1888.

His brother Khalifa, whom Barghash had once incarcerated for six years, took over but died in February 1890, his brief reign marred by outbreaks of anti-European unrest. Next in line was Khalifa's younger brother Ali, who ceded to Germany all his coastal possessions in

TOOTH AND NAIL

The word 'clove' is derived from the Latin for 'nail', which clove buds resemble, but these particular nails are rich in eugenol, which not only gives cloves their distinctive aroma but which, as an essential oil, acts as an effective local anaesthetic, especially in the relief of toothache. Chewing on a clove isn't exactly the answer to one's dental problems but eugenol might help soothe the pain until you've mortgaged the house to pay the dental fees.

Left: *Cloves are dried in the sun for four to seven days. Clove production has fallen over the last few years.*

Sultan Ali's death in 1893
caused problems regarding
the succession, for there
were three claimants: Khalid,
Hamed and Hamud. The
British intervened before
scimitars could be drawn
and appointed Hamed,
though he became little
more than a symbol. When
he did show a little independent spirit the British threatened to call in the Navy;
Hamed conveniently backed
down and died. Barghash's
son Khalid took over without
waiting for any British nod of
approval. The Royal Navy
was alerted and Khalid was
ordered to vacate the palace
by 09:00 or suffer the con-
sequences. Khalid refused
and at 09:02 precisely, with
complete lack of cultural
awareness of the Zanzibari
attitude to time, the Royal
Navy began its assault. Forty-
five minutes later 500 of
Khalid's supporters were
dead or wounded and the
'shortest war in history' was
over. Khalid fled.

return for Zanzibar becoming a British protectorate. 'If
God and the English deserted me', Ali murmured, 'my
kingdom would be doomed.' He passed away in March
1893 after years of 'continual nervous exhaustion'.

The arrival of the British administrator Gerald Portal
in 1891 must have been nervously exhausting in itself.
He denounced Zanzibar's ruling officials as 'an embodi-
ment of all the worst and most barbarous characteristics
of a primitive Arab despotism' and by the time he left,
just over a year later, he had balanced Zanzibar's books,
improved its harbour and cleaned up its filthy streets.

After Ali's succession was disputed (see fact panel) the
British installed Hamed, who soon died. The Anglophile
Hamud was then proclaimed sultan, and in 1897 signed
a decree finally making slavery illegal, though many of
the freed slaves turned to prostitution, vagrancy or
thieving. On Pemba former slaves terrorized the island.
Despite the loss of forced labour clove production actually rose, though the Arabs 'contemplated the future with
little enthusiasm while their debts increased'.

Hamud died in 1902 and the British appointed his
17-year-old son Ali, who abdicated in 1911 in favour of
Khalifa bin Harub, who reigned until his death in 1960.
Khalifa's successor and son, Abdullah, died in 1963
after having his legs amputated.

Independence

Political unrest had been simmering, however, and in
1948 there were protests by African dockyard workers
and trade unionists against their Arab and British over-
lords. In the 1950s several political parties were
allowed to form, including the Afro-Shirazi Party, the
Zanzibar and Pemba People's Party and the Zanzibar
Nationalist Party, though in a series of subsequent elections the Afro-Shirazi Party seems to have been cheated
out of office in favour of the Zanzibar Nationalists.

Jamshid bin Abdullah bin Khalifa became sultan in
1963, but a month after Zanzibar had acquired full
independence (on 10 December) a revolution took
place, during which some 13,000 men, women and

children, mostly Arabs, were slaughtered in a frenzy of ethnic cleansing by a mob of several hundred rebels, led by a migrant Ugandan labourer, John Okello, who had lived for some time in Pemba. Inspired by Okello's deranged rantings, their own hatred and greed and long-standing, understandable resentments, the rebels ran riot, raping, looting and killing.

The sultan and other lucky residents escaped, leaving behind only a tiny percentage of islanders of Arab and Indian origins. Self-styled 'Field Marshal' Okello now found himself in charge of a nation that he was incapable of governing. The Afro-Shirazi Party allied itself with the revolutionaries and its leader, Abeid Karume, who has been described as cruel and despotic despite a sometimes charming side, declared himself prime minister. In April 1964 the uneducated Karume signed away much of Zanzibar's newly won independence in a union with Julius Nyerere's mainland Tanganyika, resulting in the United Republic of Tanzania, which has never been all that united.

Under Nyerere's well-intentioned but flawed socialist idealism Tanzania, including Zanzibar, suffered economic collapse. Meanwhile, Karume, after several previous attempts on his life, was shot dead in April 1972 as he played cards in the ASP headquarters in Stone Town.

Aboud Jumbe took over and in 1977 the ASP merged with the mainland TANU to form the Chama Cha Mapinduzi party (CCM), still in power, though far from universally popular, particularly in Zanzibar. In 1985 Julius Nyerere stepped down, making way for Ali Hassan Mwinyi. Mwinyi's reforms helped to revitalize Tanzania's ruined economy and led to the country's first multi-party elections in 1995. These were bitterly contested in Zanzibar, with the CCM narrowly (and many would say unfairly) triumphing over the Civic United Front (CUF).

Salmin Amour was elected Zanzibar's president in 1995 though international observers expressed concern about the process. Further tension followed the 2000 Zanzibar elections, from which Amani Karume, son of

KEEPING IT IN THE FAMILY

Sayyid Sir Khalifa II bin Harub Al-Said, GCB, GCMG, GBE, to give him his full title, was the ninth sultan of Zanzibar. In 1900, 11 years before he came to the throne, he had married Princess Sayyida Matuka bint Hamud Al-Busaid, daughter of the seventh sultan of Zanzibar and sister of the eighth sultan, family ties among the sultans being either very close or perilously antagonistic. Another Al-Busaidi princess comes into the Khalifa picture also, for in 1922 the sultan granted a modest civil list pension to Emily Reute, formerly Princess Salme, who many years earlier had eloped with a German businessman and been banished from Zanzibar. The ex-princess, her husband long dead, had fallen upon hard times due to the fall of the German Mark after World War I. By then Emily was in her 70s and the only one of Sultan Said's many children still alive. Sadly Khalifa's generosity came too late, for his ageing relative died in Jena in 1924. Khalifa, incidentally, ruled from 1911 until 1960, making him the longest reigning of all the Zanzibari sultans.

DHOWS

As late as 1946, 678 foreign dhows came into Zanzibar, a total probably unsurpassed in East African history. But the large and beautiful *baghlahs* and *booms* (the word 'dhow' is generic and there are many specific types) have become extinct, or are almost so. *Jahazis* of over 9m (30ft) can still be seen, along with smaller *daus* and *mashuas*, the outrigger *ngalawas* and the dug-out *mtumbwis*. Dhows ply the Zanzibar Channel, carrying anything from cloves or cement to chicken feed or corrugated iron, yet few craft evoke the romance of the eastern seas more strongly, leaning into a marbled blue sea, lateen sail stretched into graceful curves by a steady monsoon.

the murdered Abeid, emerged as another disputed victor, leading to mass protests in Dar es Salaam and Zanzibar, and the deaths of at least 27 people. Mass arrests, rape and torture were alleged to have followed during a government crackdown, notably in Pemba.

The 2005 elections saw Jakya Kikwete become Tanzania's new president, whilst in Zanzibar the CCM (and Karume) again edged out the CUF to yet more violent protests, leaving the two parties as disunited as ever.

GOVERNMENT AND ECONOMY

Zanzibar is a semi-autonomous island state within the United Republic of Tanzania, its government consisting of a Revolutionary Council and House of Representatives under the leadership of an elected Zanzibari president. Elections are held concurrently with those on the mainland by direct popular vote, for similar five-year terms.

Five members of Zanzibar's House of Representatives are elected to serve on the Union's National Assembly, whose laws only affect Zanzibar in specifically designated Union matters, with Zanzibar having jurisdiction over other affairs.

Economically Zanzibar was once heavily reliant upon cloves, which, despite a declining market, still constitute a major export, together with other spices and coconut and seaweed products, but tourism is becoming the main foreign exchange earner, with annual numbers of visitors now well in excess of 100,000, and increasing.

Opposite: *A dhow sailing in Zanzibar. Dhows are still used to transport cargo – everything from cloves to cement.*

THE PEOPLE

The population of Zanzibar is about 1,000,000, many of Shirazi/Swahili descent and Swahili-speaking, though various ethnic backgrounds are represented. The people of Pemba and Tumbatu Island, however, have retained much of their subcultural individuality. About 95% of Zanzibaris are Muslims, though immigrants from the mainland (non-Muslim as well as Muslim) now live and work in Zanzibar, which has long been home to a small number of Christians (mostly of Goan or mainland African origin) and Hindus, as well as people of other backgrounds. Despite the predominance of Islam, Zanzibaris often retain vague beliefs in ancestral spirits and ghosts, and can be very superstitious.

Most native Zanzibaris are noted for their friendliness, tolerance, hospitality and good humour, despite the exacting (and in many cases increasing) poverty that most endure, though privately there are mixed views about tourism and its effects (good or bad) upon the local culture. Many Zanzibaris subsist on the proceeds from their *shambas* (smallholdings) or *dukas* (simple shops) or work in the tourism industry, clove or coconut plantations or small-scale fishing enterprises. Others, mostly women, farm seaweed and/or forage for anything edible among the rock pools of the coral shelves. A growing minority work in offices, banks, etc.

Food and Drink

Their diet, like their lifestyle, is simple. Breakfast might be sweet potatoes with chapattis, or plump triangular doughnuts (*mandazi*), taken with sugary Indian-style tea (*chai*). Midday and evening meals might consist of glutinous rice or *ugali* (a stiff maize porridge) with beans or fried fish, more

POLITICAL DIVIDE

Zanzibar's politics have always been complex and occasionally violent, though the islands are otherwise stable and their people predominantly welcoming and friendly. There is, however, a strong, underlying political divide, with supporters of the CCM (which has been in control of Zanzibar and Tanzania for many years) on one side and supporters of the opposition, the CUF, on the other. It would be easy to oversimplify the situation, but it is basically true that the CUF is particularly popular in Pemba, whilst in Unguja loyalties are more obviously split. Tensions run high at election times but otherwise tourists and other visitors, whether in Unguja or Pemba, need not worry about political differences of opinion.

SEDUCTIVE SONGS AND SMART SUITS

Taarab is to Swahili music what coconut milk is to Swahili cuisine. Just over a century ago the sultan of Zanzibar apparently sent his court musicians to Egypt and probably India to gain experience. In the process they invented and/or absorbed the style now known as *taarab*. It basically involves Arabic instruments and poignant Swahili songs of yearning and love, with a highly syncopated, seductively drowsy rhythm, which like Zanzibar itself can be hypnotic. The large male orchestras often dress in formal western dinner suits.

rarely with scrawny chicken and more rarely still with goat meat or beef. Cassava is quite popular, though not nutritious, and so are bananas (the cooking varieties are eaten in a simple stew). Savoury pancakes and a kind of spinach (*mchicha*) also form part of the regular diet, as do fish and vegetables, cooked traditionally with coconut milk.

In urban areas shoppers might snack on street or simple café food such as samosas (crispy pastry triangles stuffed with spicy minced beef or vegetables) and *mishkaki* (sticks of barbecued goat meat or beef). Sweetmeats include a gelatinous Zanzibari speciality, halva, eaten with strong black coffee (*kahawa chungu*).

Sport

Football is extremely popular among males, netball reasonably popular among girls. Surprisingly few Zanzibaris swim for pleasure. More surprisingly, perhaps, the present Minister for Sport is said to be trying to encourage cricket. Older men can often be seen engaged in the board game *bao* (see panel, page 40), or its simpler alternative, draughts. The most popular traditional music and dance is *taarab*.

The Other People (Zanzibar's Tourists)

Tourists from all over the world come to Zanzibar, many of

Below: *Worshippers on Zanzibar gather for a musical celebration at a taarab festival.*

them (don't worry if you're not among them!) honeymooners. Zanzibar's beautiful beaches (described in later chapters) are high on the list of most tourists' itineraries, together with snorkelling, diving, sport fishing and other water sports. All the best beaches in Unguja have their tourist resorts, varying from the ultra-exclusive (and expensive) to huge 'all-under-one-roof' enclosures, smaller, more select places and

Left: *Henna body art. Beautifully intricate patterns are painted onto the hands and feet.*

FORODHANI FANTASY FOOD

Almost two-thirds of Zanzibar's tourists are Italian, so you'll often see pizza on the menu. But Zanzibari pizzas (*mantabali*) are something special. They're not really pizzas, more like chubby spring rolls, made from delicious Zanzibari-style chapattis with fillings of minced meat, egg, onions or whatever else the street vendor feels like throwing in (they also do dreamy dessert pizzas with chocolate and banana).

HALVA

Halva is a gelatinous sweet-meat originating in Oman, served at times of joy or sorrow, on religious or festive occasions or merely as a symbol of traditional Zanzibari hospitality. It is made from starch, eggs, sugar, water, ghee, saffron, cardamom, nuts and sometimes rose-water. These ingredients are mixed by experienced halva-makers who can be very possessive about the details, and cooked in a large pot, used especially for the purpose, for at least two hours.

often tiny, informal Rasta places. Pemba resorts are far fewer and mostly intended for divers (and honeymooning divers) but apart from one they too can be expensive.

Tourists tend to eat in the better hotels and restaurants, where the cuisine is usually international, often with alternative, Swahili-style options. The quality of such meals varies but at its best is excellent. Seafood is obviously and deservedly popular. Less affluent or more adventurous tourists often patronize more local restaurants or cafés, where apart from the usual 'bitings' (as things such as samosas and *mishkaki* are known in East Africa) you can often get more elaborate meals, including delicious *biriani* (a favourite of the Omani sultans though it was introduced to Zanzibar by the Persian Shirazi centuries before). Your *biriani*, however, won't come with flecks of silver leaf or too much expensive saffron.

Shopping, especially among the Stone Town bazaars, is also popular with tourists, especially women. Among the gifts to look out for are colourful *kangas* (traditional cotton wraps, *see* panel page 96), Arabian-style perfumes such as *oud* (*see* panel page 7), woven baskets and mats, Zanzibar chests, antiques (though most of the best ones have gone long ago), spices in attractive, woven presentation dishes, *tinga-tinga* paintings (very much a personal preference or not, *see* page 63), blackwood ('ebony') carvings and of course books on Zanzibar, including Swahili/Zanzibari recipes.

2
Stone Town

Stone Town is the old quarter of Zanzibar Town. It is essentially 19th century, and although many of its buildings have been allowed to crumble, its disarmingly higgledy-piggledy layout and East-meets-West character would still ring bells with Sultan Barghash or Henry Morton Stanley. And maybe with Richard Burton, who in typically deprecating prose described it as 'a filthy labyrinth, a capricious arabesque of disorderly lanes, and alleys, and impasses, here broad, there narrow; now heaped with offal, then choked with ruins'. The kind of place he obviously loved. As will you. To lose oneself in its labyrinth is not just an exciting adventure into the romance (and occasionally the decadence) of the 'mystic East' but a translocation in time.

Losing oneself, on foot, is the best way to get to know it. You won't be lost for long and in any case, who minds being lost in such fascinating surroundings? 'Fascinating' is a word to be wary of in travel guides, but anyone who is not fascinated by Stone Town must have the curiosity of a sea-cucumber or, to be more charitable, be in need of a good guide. The sense of history, the architecture with its Islamic simplicity on the one hand and intricate Indian prodigality on the other, and Stone Town's greatest charm, its cultural kaleidoscope of people, are enough to enthral the most world-weary of travellers.

THE WATERFRONT

Stone Town's **waterfront** is among the most historic in the world, best seen in panorama from the sea. A leisurely stroll along its length, however, will give you a more intimate

DON'T MISS

★★★ Losing yourself in the **bazaars** and narrow **streets**, people-watching, etc.
★★ Visiting the **Cathedral Church of Christ**, site of the old slave market.
★★ **Palace** and **House of Wonders** museums.
★★ **Forodhani** street-food market.
★★ **Sunsets**, silhouetted **dhows** and **sundowners** at Shangani Point (from the Africa House Terrace, Serena or Tembo House).

Opposite: *Cathedral Church of Christ, built over the former slave market.*

Above: *The People's Palace Museum is the former Sultan's Palace.*

view and, unless you stop off on the way, take you little more than half an hour. Stopping off (distractions are a way of life in Zanzibar) is not a bad thing, as you will find.

Assuming you have arrived by ferry, a short detour will bring you to the **old dhow harbour**, just east of the landing stage and the dockyard complex, built by the British in 1925 on reclaimed land. The harbour is no longer a forest of masts and the majestic ocean-going dhows are now seldom seen, but you should see a few coastal *jahazis*, the largest dhows still operating in the region.

The Old Dispensary

Almost opposite the dockyard entrance/exit gate is the **Old Dispensary** ('the Old' in Zanzibar being used as freely as 'ye Olde' in 'Merrie England'). The building is one of Stone Town's finest, in the ecstatically over-the-top Indian manner. Its double-decker balconies seem to have been carved by craftsmen intoxicated by their own expertise, an orderly clutter of intricate balustrades, fretwork and fascia boards, the whole upper frontage supported by columns and elegantly carved brackets. The interior is almost as ornate.

Built as a hospital, it was the inspiration of **Tharia Topan**, a prominent Ismaili merchant of Indian origin. Topan laid the foundation stone himself in 1887, appropriately with a golden trowel, to mark Queen Victoria's Golden Jubilee, but died in India in 1891 before it was completed. As well as being head of customs and advisor to the sultan he was also, it seems, banker to the infamous slave trader Tippu Tip. After Topan's death his widow funded the building's completion and in 1900 it was bought as a charitable dispensary. Like other buildings in Stone Town it was grievously neglected after the revolution, to be rescued by the Aga Khan Trust for Culture during the 1990s, re-opening as a cultural centre, though it presently languishes a little, as if trying to recover a sense of purpose.

Moving on you soon pass (to your right) the popular **Mercury's Restaurant and Bar**, overlooking the harbour and named after **Freddie Mercury**, the stage name of the late Zanzibar-born musician. Almost opposite is a big tree, known as (wait for it) the **Big Tree**, a fine Indian banyan planted by Sultan Khalifa bin Harub in 1911. Its crown sometimes provides refuge for a family of vervet monkeys, as well as acting as a giant green parasol for the craftsmen who build small dhows beneath.

Just beyond the Big Tree to landward is the **Seaview Restaurant** and beyond the intervening alleyway the **Old Customs House**, with its weathered Zanzibar door and sedately appealing exterior. Its upper floor is occupied by the **Dhow Countries Music Academy**, which welcomes visitors to official or impromptu sessions.

The Sultan's Palace

Further along is the former Sultan's Palace, currently in need of a make-over and known officially as the **People's Palace**. It is an unimposing but attractive structure in the Arab style, its whitewashed walls penetrated by Islamic arches at ground level and a series of long rectangular windows along the second storey, with an open *baraza* to one side and crenellated parapets and red-tile roofs above. One or two palms lend their usual grace to the overall effect.

MERCURIAL MUSICIAN

Freddie Mercury is to Stone Town what the Beatles are to Liverpool; everyone over a certain age went to school with him or lived 'next door'. In fact, Freddie (a Parsee, real name Farok Bulsara) left Zanzibar aged nine, for boarding school in India, later studying at Ealing College in London. He found fame as lead singer of the rock group Queen but died of AIDS in 1991. Mercury's Restaurant and Bar in Stone Town is his spiritual memorial.

A MODEL FATHER

Said's daughter Salme, who inherited some of her father's risk-taking spirit (she eloped with a German businessman), remembered Said as 'a model father', going on to say: 'Justice he valued as the highest of all things, and in this respect he knew no difference of person, not even one between one of his own sons and the lowest of his slaves. He humbled himself before God, and he was not conceited and proud like so many highborn people.'

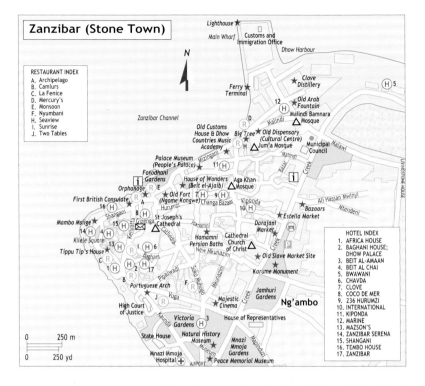

Zanzibar (Stone Town)

RESTAURANT INDEX
A. Archipelago
B. Camlurs
C. La Fenice
D. Mercury's
E. Monsoon
F. Nyumbani
H. Seaview
I. Sunrise
J. Two Tables

HOTEL INDEX
1. AFRICA HOUSE
2. BAGHANI HOUSE;
   DHOW PALACE
3. BEIT AL-AMAAN
4. BEIT AL CHAI
5. BWAWANI
6. CHAVDA
7. CLOVE
8. COCO DE MER
9. 236 HURUMZI
10. INTERNATIONAL
11. KIPONDA
12. MARINE
13. MAZSON'S
14. ZANZIBAR SERENA
15. SHANGANI
16. TEMBO HOUSE
17. ZANZIBAR

The palace stands on the site of Sultan Said's original *Beit el-Sahel* (House of the Coast). It is now a museum, housing such furniture and household possessions that the last sultan left behind when he fled for his life, and which were not carted away by the rebels or their political successors. The museum gives some idea of the tastes and lifestyles of the later sultans, though its most interesting room is dedicated to Said's rather unconventional daughter **Salme**, even though she never lived in this palace, which was built in the late 1890s. On the eastern side of the palace is the royal graveyard, where sultans Said and Barghash, among others, lie buried.

Said's original palace had been seriously damaged in 1896, during the 'shortest war in history', and the Royal Navy had also shelled the **Beit el-Hukm** (House of

Government), which then stood between the palace and the *Beit el-Ajaib* (House of Wonders). For a service that prides itself on chivalry towards damsels in distress this particular bit of demolition was rather ungallant, as the *Beit el-Hukm* was said to contain more women than men, and was often referred to as the palace harem; one hopes that the ladies were safely evacuated. The bombardment also destroyed a nearby clock tower.

The site of the House of Government is now a sequestered little sanctuary of elegant palms, often overlooked by passing tourists, as the garden itself is overlooked, in a different sense, by the adjacent **Beit el-Ajaib**, Sultan Barghash's House of Wonders. This building is said to occupy the site of a 17th-century palace belonging to Queen Fatuma binti Hasan, who following the Omani take-over paid for supporting the Portuguese by a decade's exile in Muscat.

The *Beit el-Ajaib* was once, by royal insistence as well as planning, the highest building in Zanzibar (and East Africa) and is still the highest building in Stone Town. It was the first building in the region to have electricity and running water and even an electrically operated lift, long out of order, though funds are currently being sought to elevate it to its former glory.

Its doors are suitably wondrous works of art, in traditional Zanzibar style, which wasn't Zanzibari at all. Barghash, whom the British had once banished to their 'naughty corner' in Bombay, had returned to Zanzibar full of admiration for some of the architectural features he had seen. He is said to have brought an Indian master craftsman over to carve the new palace doors. The results

Below: *A view of the House of Wonders in Stone Town.*

Above: *The Old Fort was erected after the Portuguese were expelled from Zanzibar.*

were so splendid that they were copied by local door-makers, whose work may still be seen here and there throughout the town.

The *Beit el-Ajaib* was largely undamaged by the naval bombardment in 1896, though hit by a few shells. It too is now a museum, very well laid out and informative, its exhibits portraying and explaining, among others, various aspects of Zanzibari and Swahili culture. Two Portuguese cannon, cast in bronze in the 16th century, stand outside the palace's main door, close to where cages containing lions and other animals, presented to the sultan by various well-wishers, once stood.

The Old Fort

Next in line is the **Old Fort** (*Ngome Kongwe*), a rather squat edifice composed of four coral ragstone walls with cylindrical towers at the corners and a fifth in the centre of the southernmost. A faded golden brown in colour, it was erected by the Omanis immediately after expelling the Portuguese from Zanzibar in 1698. Only the ruins of a chapel, dating back to around 1600, and an adjacent merchant's house remain from the Portuguese period. Never more than a basic structure, and lightly garrisoned (in 1710 by as few as 50 men), it saw little military action, though in 1754 it withstood an attack by the Mazrui and in 1784 helped in subduing civil disturbances.

After Sultan Said's move to Zanzibar in 1832 the fort served as a prison, and in 1946 the British turned it into a club for women of all communities, many of them in purdah. Despite the encumbrance of their Islamic clothing, the Muslim women apparently joined the rest in games of tennis, badminton and basketball in the fort's grounds. Less ladylike pursuits took place beyond the eastern wall, for criminals were publicly beheaded here by the sword, the last executions taking place in 1890. Happier public events are now held on the inner side of the same wall, where an open-air amphitheatre is the setting for live concerts, including two of Zanzibar's most popular annual festivals (see panel, page 32). There is a restaurant and bar within the grounds, a simple outdoor place in which to escape the heat and bustle of the town, and a collection of kiosks selling gifts and souvenirs.

Forodhani Gardens

Between the fort and the sea lies an expanse of lawns and trees, the **Forodhani Gardens**. Forodhani means 'unloading place' and it was here that many slave dhows discharged their unfortunate cargoes. The gardens come into their own in late afternoon, when the sun's intensity becomes less so and young men, full of vitality after their various daytime activities, entertain visitors with impromptu diving displays from the sea wall. It is then that Forodhani's excellent street-food market is set up to cater, until well into the evening, to the throngs of tourists who are attracted to it. Hopefully, after current renovations to the gardens, the stalls will regain their former prominence and hopefully the authorities will do something to deter the touts and hangers-on (known as papasi or ticks) who can be quite a nuisance here and elsewhere.

Treasury Passage

The route now proceeds through or around a road tunnel, known as **Treasury Passage** as the buildings above it once formed the sultans' treasury. Before entering the tunnel (or the quieter lane to one side), however, it is worth glancing to one's left, along the western wall of the fort, to the two buildings just beyond the far tower. Both buildings now belong to the People's Bank of Zanzibar, but in the 1860s one (presumably the taller building on the right) housed **Princess Salme**, daughter of Sultan Said, and the other housed a German businessman, Heinrich Reute. Salme was in her early twenties, both parents dead, and

UNWELCOME IMMIGRANT

The Indian house crow (Corvus splendens) was introduced to Zanzibar from India over a century ago, apparently by misguided British civil servants (who assumed it would help keep Stone Town clear of edible litter). They were right in this assumption but underestimated the crow's rapacious, domineering nature. It has now spread to the mainland, in some cases far inland, devastating indigenous bird life in many towns and cities.

Above: *A crucifix in the Cathedral Church of Christ, made from the wood of the tree under which Livingstone's heart was buried in 1857.*

LIONIZED CELEBRITY

On its arrival in Zanzibar the coffin containing David Livingstone's remains was taken upstairs in the old British Consulate. In a room still used as an office it was opened and a surgeon inspected what was left of the crudely embalmed body, now unrecognizable. The surgeon identified it by the faulty articulation of the left shoulder, crushed by the jaws of a lion in 1843 (Livingstone had cleaned the wound by stuffing maggots into it to eat the putrifying flesh).

recently returned from internal exile for her (minor) part in a palace plot in support of her brother Barghash.

A barred window in her house overlooked the flat roof next door, and the curious princess, intrigued by the Western customs such as dinner parties that she observed from a few metres away, became friendly with Reute. Extremely friendly, in fact; she became pregnant by him. In most Arab countries this could have led to her being stoned to death. Fortunately the British were already a power behind the throne in Zanzibar and the daring princess, with the help of John Kirk, the British consul, and his wife, was spirited away to Aden by the Royal Navy, which claims that it 'never says no to a lady'. The ship was appropriately called *HMS Highflyer*, for Salme was something of a free spirit.

Her baby was born in Aden that December (1866) and the following May her faithful lover arrived. The two were married and Salme became a Christian and was baptized (as Emily) in the same morning; Zanzibaris might be laid-back but once they do get going they don't mess about. The couple settled in Germany and had three more children, but the fairy tale did not have the customary happy ending… Heinrich was knocked down and killed by a tram in 1870. Salme lived on in Germany and later Beirut, dying of pneumonia in Jena in 1924 at the age of 80. A small bag of sand from the beach by her beloved Mtoni Palace was found among her possessions, and even more poignantly, the dress she had worn during her elopement. The bag of sand was buried with her ashes in Heinrich's grave.

In the **Treasury Passage** vicinity are several small **cafés**, and the waterfront road now bends around into Shangani Street, out of sight of the sea. On the junction of Shangani Street and Kenyatta Road, to seaward, stands the **first British Consulate** (1841–74), a large, chunky building reminiscent, from outside, of a somewhat ramshackle Arab mansion, and marked by a circular and much-faded sign on its eastern wall. As the sign announces, 'Here at different times lived **Speke**, **Burton**, **Grant** and **Kirk**. **David Livingstone** stayed here and in this house his body rested on its long journey home'.

Livingstone's 'long journey home' had begun in the Bangweulu Wetlands of what is now northern Zambia. After a journey of nine months his body was brought to Bagamoyo (on the Tanzanian coast opposite Zanzibar) by a party of faithful servants and others, placed in a proper coffin and shipped across the Straits courtesy of *HMS Vulture* (the missionary-explorer, despite his dour Scottish image, had a good sense of humour and would have surely enjoyed the unintended joke).

Just around the corner from the old British Consulate stands the **Tembo House Hotel**, formerly the home of an Asian businessman and before that the **American Consulate**. **Henry Morton Stanley**, an American citizen for a while, would have stayed and/or been entertained here.

The last important building along the Mizingani-Shangani waterfront, known as ***Mambo Msiige*** (Without Equal), is best seen from the beach just west of the Tembo House Hotel's seaside terrace. It is another large block of a building in simple Arab style, its uppermost storey obviously an afterthought said to have been added for the personal use of Henry Morton Stanley. At one time (1864–74) it was the local headquarters of the Universities Mission to Central Africa, an ironic situation as they were there primarily to help stop the slave trade, and slaves had reputedly been buried alive in the walls of *Mambo Msiige* during its construction in the mid-1800s, presumably to bring good luck upon the house. This practice is said to have been common at that time (*see* panel, page 16).

Below: *The interior of the Tembo House Hotel.*

TIPPU TIP

Hamed bin Mohammed el Murjebi, known as Tippu Tip (because of a nervous tic in one eye), was the most notorious of the Zanzibari slave traders. His autobiography expresses no remorse for his long involvement in slavery but he was, nevertheless, a tough, courageous and resourceful man. Several explorers travelled with him at times, notably Henry Morton Stanley, who thought him 'a remarkable man' with a 'fine, intelligent face' and impeccable manners.

INSIDE STONE TOWN
Shangani, Place of Beads

Stone Town was designed to keep out heat (almost synonymous with light in the coastal tropics) and, one might think, to keep entranced, if sometimes bewildered, outsiders from escaping. Its most popular area is **Shangani** (Place of Beads), where Stone Town probably began.

Shangani Point is the westernmost extremity of the Stone Town triangle. Creek Road, to the east, forms the base, marking the alignment of a creek that according to Richard Burton once exhaled a night-time miasma that 'causes candles to burn dim and which changes the sound of the human voice'. Shangani Point is now occupied by the **Zanzibar Serena Hotel**, the main sector of which was once the Cable and Wireless building, once connected to Aden by telegraphic cable. Skeletons, perhaps of more poor slaves buried alive, were discovered in the original foundations during the 1990s (see panel, page 16). The smaller section of the Serena was originally the '**Chinese Doctor's House**'.

Apart from the skeletons that were unearthed during its construction the Serena overlooks the original Zanzibar slave market, now one of Stone Town's quietest corners, yet it is known as **Kilele (Noise) Square**. The name recalls the time when the old slave market was replaced by one dealing in vegetables, with vendors yelling out to proclaim, presumably, the superiority of their radishes or sweet potatoes.

Close to the southern corner of Kilele Square, in a narrow lane leading to the intriguingly named **Suicide Alley**, is **Tippu Tip's House** (ask if you cannot find it). Sadly, its interior has been allowed to crumble (one wonders why) but its doorway is one of the most evocative in Stone Town. Through that doorway, between his years-long expeditions, walked Zanzibar's most notorious slave trader and, one assumes, his 35 or so wives and approximately 90 concubines, whom, we are told, he 'continued to pleasure' into his seventies. Despite his ruthless occupation he was an adventurous, sophisticated man. The house, needless to say, is haunted.

Just up the lane is the **Africa House Hotel**, recently restored and with its own splendid door. It was built in 1888 as an exclusively English club, though eventually other Europeans and even Americans were allowed in to lend a different slant to the conversation about the weather and the difficulty in finding decent servants. Its members would have choked on their gin and tonics had they known that the terrace would one day be popular with package tourists, backpackers and other 'non-U' hoi polloi, bathed in the glow of the glorious sunsets and (damn their insolence) having a frightfully good time.

The eastern boundary of Shangani is Kenyatta Road. Its intersection with Shangani Street is one of the busiest in Stone Town, and like the rest of Shangani, well-provided with cafés, hotels and gift shops. A little way south of the intersection is the **Old Post Office**, still in use. Built in 1906 and designed by the distinguished British architect John Sinclair (*see* panel, this page), it is a colonnaded structure in green and white which, by accident or design, are colours often associated with Islam.

There are several attractive old buildings along Kenyatta and on the right as you proceed south, close to the point where it merges with Kaunda Road, is **General**

Above: *The crumbling house of Tippu Tip.*

SEDUCED BY THE EAST

John Sinclair was a British architect trained in Classical forms but seduced by the East into what is now known as the Saracenic style, a mostly happy, idiosyncratic marriage of Islamic East and neoclassical West. He came to Zanzibar, ironically, just after the Royal Navy had rearranged some of Stone Town's architectural assets during the 'shortest war in history'. As if to make amends for this lack of cultural awareness, Sinclair soon began to design more enduring and memorable buildings, in the Saracenic manner.

'A VERY PECULIAR MAN'

Richard Burton's wife once confessed that she had 'undertaken a very peculiar man'. She certainly had. Burton was fascinated by the East, its sensations, horrors, brothels and erotica (he translated the *Arabian Nights*, the *Kama Sutra* and the *Perfumed Garden*, as well as two volumes of Latin poetry, six of Portuguese literature and four books of international folk tales). He was an author himself, a brilliant linguist (29 languages), a soldier, swordsman, archaeologist, zoologist, geologist, botanist, ethnologist, raconteur, amateur physician and (later) a diplomat. He was also, of course, an explorer.

Lloyd Matthews' House, presently a dentist's surgery. Patients might distract themselves from more immediate anxieties by lying back and thinking of the Empire, for Lloyd Matthews was one of the British Empire's most loyal servants, and a good friend to Sultan Barghash. An ex-naval lieutenant, he was seconded to the sultan's army as Major General, and to everyone's surprise, probably including his, succeeded in transforming the largely Baluchi soldiery ('disciplined only by their own fears' in the words of Richard Burton) into an effective fighting force.

Kaunda Road

Close to where Kenyatta Road becomes Kaunda Road is the so-called **Portuguese Arch**, though why Portuguese is a mystery that need not detain you. A more worthy structure stands across the road, though most of the people who visit it have more on their minds than its architectural merits, for it is Zanzibar's **High Court**. Built between 1904 and 1908, it is a fine example of Sinclair's work, with characteristically Islamic features (including the Moorish arch over the main door), pleasing proportions and a domed tower.

Further south, on the same seaward side of the road, is another of Sinclair's buildings, the whitewashed, red-roofed **State House**, official home of the president of Zanzibar, formerly that of the British Resident. Photography is forbidden, which is a pity as it is an attractive building with British colonial as well as Arabic implications, best seen from the sea.

Directly across from it are the **Victoria Gardens and Hall**, established by Sultan Barghash for the pleasure of his harem. It contained baths, since covered over. In 1887, on the occasion of Queen Victoria's Golden Jubilee, it was presented to the people of Zanzibar by Sultan Hamud. A botanical garden, including exotics such as tea, coffee and cocoa, was established using plants taken from John Kirk's old garden at Mbweni.

At the far end of the gardens, still heading south, you can fork left into Museum Road, which brings you to another of Sinclair's buildings, the **Peace Memorial Museum**, its name commemorating the dead of World War I. Inspired by the Aya Sofya Mosque in Istanbul, with six hexagonal domes supporting the much larger main dome in the centre, and some gracefully barred and arched windows, it was completed in 1925 after Sinclair's official retirement. It is one of his most interest-

Above: *The Peace Memorial Museum commemorates those who died in World War I.*

ing creations, though its exhibits have been transferred elsewhere and it is now in need of a Fairy Godmother to restore its self-belief.

Yet another of Sinclair's works, though not in this area, is the **Bharmal Building** at the far end of Creek Road. Built for a local Asian merchant, its appearance is more Indian than Arabic, with moulded stucco and coloured glass windows (an Indian embellishment common in many Stone Town buildings). It was built in 1923, towards the end of his career, and is a rather garish contrast to the Peace Memorial Museum erected soon afterwards.

Stone Town's Bazaars

There are many buildings and some wonderful old doors in Stone Town but the greatest attraction for most visitors are its **bazaars**, not only for the *dukas* (shops) themselves, but for the atmosphere and multicultural buzz of the narrow lanes. It is a place of stark contrasts, not least in terms of light and shadow, and as if to emphasize Livingstone's remark about Unguja ('...an illusive place where nothing is as it seems'), the intruder is overwhelmed by what appears to be a mysteriously medieval experience, despite the fact that the town is essentially 19th century.

WELL-DEVELOPED CHESTS

Beautifully crafted Zanzibar chests, some quite old, are to be seen in many hotels and resorts throughout Unguja, as well as in the Stone Town bazaars. They actually originated in Persia and India (Bombay and Surat), each area having its own distinct style, though they also became popular (ready-made) in Arabia. The best of them are crafted from teak and exquisitely decorated with perforated brass roundels, studs and strengthening straps.

BAO

Bao (Swahili for 'board') is a popular board game in Zanzibar and mainland Tanzania, believed to be the most complicated of the Mancala family of games played in many parts of Africa, and perhaps one of the oldest board games in the world. Boards are dimpled with even rows of shallow, circular depressions (mashimo) in which counters (kete) are placed, the aim of the game being to capture your opponent's counters through strategic moves.

The two most popular bazaars are those that almost parallel the waterfront, passing behind the Old Fort, beginning (or ending) with **Gizenga Street**, which branches off from Kenyatta Road in Shangani, close to the Old Post Office. The eastern end of Gizenga emerges by the extreme southeastern tower of the fort, where you should bear right into **Hurumzi Street**, ignoring its sudden left turn and proceeding straight on along **Changa Bazaar**. Of course you don't need to stick rigidly to this route; you can get lost (and probably will) wherever the fancy takes you. Another interesting route is along the initially very narrow **Cathedral Street**, which takes you past the suitably Romanesque frontage of **St Joseph's Roman Catholic Cathedral**, designed by M Berangier, architect of Notre Dame de la Garde of Marseilles. The first Mass was performed here on Christmas night, 1898. Cathedral Street leads straight on to become **Soko Muhogo** (Cassava Market) Street.

Many of the *dukas* in the bazaars are now tourist-orientated, but among the gift and souvenir shops you will still find some selling fruits, vegetables or groceries, spices or perfumes, colourful *kangas* (cotton wraps), old clocks, medicines, hardware or Zanzibar chests. Chests are sometimes set out on the *barazas*, the solid stone benches that border the lanes, though more often the *barazas* are reserved for locals to sit on and watch the world go by, or for the display of fruits and vegetables.

Watching the world go by is Stone Town's greatest pleasure. People of almost any nationality, religion and racial complexion might pass, but perhaps the Zanzibaris, for most of us, are the most exciting. You do not need a doctorate in genetics to see traces of certain ethnic origins among them, from paler, fine-featured Arab, Persian and Indian faces to softer, darker African ones. Descendants of slaves and no doubt slave traders, sultans and minor merchant princes pass each other on the street or perhaps play *bao* together at Stone Town's little social nodes, those gathering places at odd corners of the narrow lanes. Here and there will be hints of Far Eastern or European genealogy, just to keep you on your toes, or confuse you even more.

Clothes are often a give-away: perhaps an Omani-style turban, an Indian sari or the blouse, skirt and uncovered head of a Christian Goan girl, though Islam is predominant. Muslim men often wear casual western clothes, but rarely without the *kofia*, an embroidered Muslim cap. Some, especially on Fridays, still wear the traditional white ankle-length *kanzu*. Muslim women will normally wear the *buibui* (the long outer garment, often black but with the latest trend in patterning or trimmings) with fashionable Western clothes beneath. The *hijab* (headscarf) worn by most of them might be black or white or any colour of the spectrum. A few women will be in full purdah, only eyes and occasionally ankles visible to the onlooker. Many Muslim women of Bantu origin favour the *kanga* or brightly coloured African wrap, with one piece doubling as a headscarf.

Above: *Coffee is served – thick, black and strong.*

Zanzibari women, especially those of Arab or Persian descent, will usually remain politely aloof, often shielding their faces from passing men by drawing one side of their *hijab* across their faces with a practised movement of the hand. Their right to privacy should be respected, here or elsewhere, and photographs, however tempting, should not be taken without permission. It will rarely be given unless you know the women personally, or are with some-one who does.

Except during the holy month of Ramadan you will see the occasional coffee vendor, or someone selling *mishkaki* (sticks of barbecued meat) and chapattis, or sugar cane juice, straight from the hand-operated press. You will certainly see (and sometimes have to sidestep with the dexterity of a matador) a succession of bicycles, motorbikes,

BLACK ADRENALIN

Stone Town's traditional coffee sellers still patrol the bazaars with their pots of *kahawa chungu* (bitter coffee) and little trays of tiny cups, all carried by means of a yoke across the shoulders. Sadly, many of the old conical brass pots have been sold to antique shops or hotels and replaced by aluminium kettles, and many coffee sellers now hang around popular intersections rather than risk branding the odd tourist bottom with their little pans of hot charcoal.

scooters, mopeds and handcarts. They can be irritating but they are part of the overall charm, and without the tinkle of bells, the splutter of two-stroke engines and the soft rumble and rattle of carts Stone Town would not be quite the same.

The Buildings of Inner Stone Town

Most buildings are Omani or northwest Indian in style. The Omani's house, even more than the Englishman's, was his castle, a square-built, multistoreyed block of coral stone, its exterior plain except for a few panels of incised stuccowork and the all-important door, and penetrated by a regular series of small windows, those on the ground floor barred. Stone *barazas* would normally be placed on either side of the door. Within there would often be a central courtyard, the family living in the upper rooms around it, their womenfolk shielded from public gaze by broad verandahs and pillars. In contrast to the stark exterior it would often be lavishly furnished.

Below: *The Cathedral Church of Christ is built in a mixture of architectural styles.*

Many Indian buildings began as simple hole-in-the-wall *dukas*, reflecting the poverty of most early Indian settlers. The door would be in four-leaf Gujarati style, decorated with a multitude of recessed square panels. As fortunes rose, so did the houses, storey by storey, starting with the first conversion into a typical Indian *uppar makan*, *niche dukan* (home above, shop below). Elaborate wooden upper balconies were added, with ornate fretworked embellishments.

Houses of these two main types may be seen everywhere in Stone Town, many converted into hotels, but among the town's most interesting buildings are its mosques, churches and temples. St Joseph's Cathedral has already been mentioned but a more famous one stands a short walk to the east, in Mkunazini; if you don't get lost, that is, for its spire is rarely visible and you can be quite close to it without realizing. It is the **Cathedral Church of Christ**, famous not for its grandeur but its location, for it stands on the site of Zanzibar's most notorious **slave market**.

Its interior is more becoming than the austere and disproportionate outer shell. Behind the font a **stained-glass window** commemorates the British sailors who died on anti-slavery patrols, and on a pillar at one side of the chancel is a **crucifix** made from the tree under which Livingstone's heart was buried, close to where he died, during the night whilst kneeling in prayer. The **altar** stands where the whipping post of the slave market once stood. The cathedral's construction was overseen by **Bishop Steere**, who every Friday (the Islamic holy day) had the Victorian cheek to preach Christianity to Muslims in the adjoining chapel.

When the Sunday morning service is in full swing, the voices of the choir blending into a moving, particularly African timbre, the cathedral dignitaries in their black and scarlet and white robes, it is humbling to stand behind the congregation and take it all in. And more humbling, perhaps, to sit outdoors, where once, from about four o'clock each afternoon, the **slaves** would have sat or stood. Children, popular because they would hopefully live longer and be more tractable, were displayed in the centre of the market, adult men elsewhere and women in their own area, forming several semicircles. Women would have their bodies 'painted', in the words of Royal Naval officer Captain Smee, 'with barely a yard of cloth around their hips, with rows of girls from the age of around twelve and upwards exposed to the examination of throngs of Arabs, and subject to inexpressible indignities by the brutal dealers'. The girls and women would often be made to strip naked. Slave chambers near the square's entrance bring home, more tangibly, 'man's inhumanity to man'.

The humiliations observed by Smee were nothing compared with the abuses and atrocities that slaves sometimes

VERTICALLY CHALLENGED CHURCH

The Cathedral Church of Christ was begun in 1873, the year the slave market closed. Basilican in type and a mixture of Gothic and Arabic in style, its roof is made of Portland cement and crushed coral. The result is not too alluring, thanks partly to Sultan Barghash, who donated the cathedral's clock on condition that the church's spire did not exceed the height of his House of Wonders. The spire is consequently absurdly small compared with the hefty bulk of the nave.

TWO SIDES OF THE BRITISH COIN

Many British merchants and entrepreneurs profited from the trafficking of slaves (in Britain's case the West African trade), as did merchants and entrepreneurs from a host of other countries. But Britain, through such men as Hamilton, Livingstone, Kirk, Bartle Frere and many others, played a major part in the ending of the East African trade. Men of the British Royal Navy, committed to anti-slaving patrols off the East African coast, performed with great professionalism and courage, despite being faced by near-impossible odds in often exacting circumstances. They saved hundreds, perhaps thousands, of people from cruel voyages to the Gulf or elsewhere, and from lifetimes of slavery once they got there. Many British sailors died on such patrols, mostly of disease but sometimes in battles with the slave dhow crews.

Opposite: *The Darajani Market in Stone Town sells fruit, vegetables, fish and meat.*

suffered, especially (though not only) in Portuguese East Africa, where slaves who were deemed to have committed serious offences might be broken on the wheel, a heinous form of torture and execution, and in clement weather take three days or so to die, and where having an ear or one's nose cut off was a minor punishment. Prices of slaves varied. Children were valued for their youth (which often ensured years of service), their greater adaptability and in certain cases their emergent sexual attractiveness. Stanley noted that teenage girls in Ujiji in 1876 fetched up to four times as much as an adult male. But a missionary based by Lake Nyasa in 1871 said he had seen children between eight and ten bought for less corn than would fit into a hat.

Another, quite different market stands close to the cathedral, alongside Creek Road, though it too hardly smells of roses. It is the **Darajani Market**, dealing in fruit, vegetables, fish and meat. Its vegetarian sectors are interesting and wholesome. The others are more interesting but not for the weak-at-heart. Carcasses, not always immediately identifiable, hang from hooks, attended by dopy flies, while fishmongers beat octopuses into oblivion with stones or hack the fins from bleeding sharks. The smell does little for the appetite.

Wherever you are in Stone Town you are never far from a mosque, though surprisingly minarets (the towers often associated with mosques) are uncommon. One exception is the minaret (added relatively recently) of the old **Ibadhi Mosque** that rises above the Gizenga Street bazaar. Another is the elliptical minaret of Stone Town's oldest (17th-century) mosque, the **Malindi Bamnara**. The town's largest mosque, one of its most beautiful, is the **Jum'a (Friday) Mosque** at Mizingani, just behind the Big Tree. Most mosques are deliberately functional in style but those of the more liberal sects often have attractive embellishments, especially in terms of the arch of the mihrab, the niche from where the Imam leads the prayers, and sometimes roof-supporting arches. One example is the mihrab of the Barza Mosque at Mkunazini, whilst the **Ismaili Jama'at Khana**, in Hurumzi, has a fine Gujarati-style door.

Among Zanzibar's various temples, which include a Zoroastrian fire temple and a Buddhist temple, a tribute to the religious tolerance of the isles, the **Shiva Shakti Hindu Temple**, behind the Palace complex, is the most accessible for tourists. Its three towers are a familiar Stone Town landmark when seen from the roofs of convenient buildings, though like the church spires, rarely visible from street level. Respectful non-Hindus are welcome.

Among other noteworthy buildings are the **Hamamni Persian Baths** in the town centre. Commissioned by the public-minded Sultan Barghash in the early 1870s, they were designed in simple but relatively elegant Persian style, for the use of Stone Town's citizens, proceeds going to a charitable trust. The coolness within their thick stone walls, and the baths themselves (no longer in use), must have been more than welcome in Zanzibar's southern summer. They are still cool, in the physical if not the colloquial sense, but disappointed visitors will have the satisfaction of knowing that their admission fees go to the Zanzibar Orphanage.

THE ZANZIBAR CHRISTMAS TREE

Towns in Zanzibar, like others throughout the tropics, have many exotic trees and shrubs, planted for their shade and/or decorative blossoms. One of the most striking is that splendid native of Madagascar, the flamboyant, one of several 'flame trees'. It is at its best towards December, when its scarlet blossoms contrast gloriously with the feathery, bright green leaves. The time of year and 'Christmassy' colour combination have earned the flamboyant its colloquial name, the Zanzibar Christmas tree.

Stone Town at a Glance

Mid-June to mid-October, when temperatures and humidity are lowest and rainfall usually minimal, is in many ways the best time to go to Zanzibar. Mid-March to mid-May can be quite wet and very humid and is usually best avoided. Mid-December to mid-March can sometimes be uncomfortably hot and humid, sometimes with rain, but this period should not be discounted, especially if you are in Zanzibar for diving.

GETTING THERE

Most international airlines do not fly directly into Zanzibar, for which the main gateways by air are **Dar es Salaam International Airport** (mainland coast), **Kilimanjaro International Airport** (northern Tanzania; often used by tourists combining Zanzibar with a safari) and **Nairobi International Airport** (Kenya), also used by many people combining Zanzibar with a wildlife safari. Many **international airlines** serve these airports. Onward flights to **Zanzibar International Airport** (Unguja) are available through Air Tanzania, Ethiopian Airlines, Gulf Air, Kenya Airlines and **private, domestic-based airlines** including Coastal Air, Precision Air and Zan Air. Flight times between Dar and Zanzibar airport are only about 20 minutes but make allowances for getting to and

from airports and for the usual waiting around in departure lounges. Several **ferries** operate from the terminal opposite St Joseph's Cathedral on the Dar waterfront (see Useful Contacts). Ignore touts at the ferry terminal as they are looking for commission, and check departure times in advance as they can change at short notice. Ferries take around one-and-a-half to two hours, depending on the ferry and sea conditions.

GETTING AROUND

The best way to see Stone Town is on foot, though you can hire taxis to and from the airport or docks, or to ferry you around the outer limits of the town (haggle beforehand, not afterwards). You might also be able to hire bicycles.

WHERE TO STAY

LUXURY
236 Hurumzi, tel: (0)777 423 266, (0)777 438 020, www.emerson-green.com Formerly Emerson and Green's. Charmingly redesigned and one of East Africa's top hotels. Situated in Hurumzi, behind the old Sultan's Palace complex.
Africa House Hotel, Shangani, tel: (0)777 432 340. Historical hotel. Views of sea and sunsets from terrace.
Beit al Chai, tel: (0)777 444 111. Pleasant, converted three-storey old tea house by Kilele Square (once a slave

market) in Shangani.
Tembo House Hotel, tel: (0)24 223 3005/2609, email: tembo@zitec.org www. tembohotel.com Originally the old American Consulate. Elaborately furnished in traditional Zanzibari style, excellent location on main waterfront by Shangani Point. Best rooms in original sector, overlooking sea. No alcohol.
Zanzibar Serena Hotel, tel: (0)24 223 1015. Listed among the Best Small Hotels of the World. Excellent location on Shangani Point.

MID-RANGE
Baghani House, tel: (0)22 223 5654. Next to Dhow Palace, imaginatively furnished in authentic Zanzibari style and popular, especially with families.
Beit al-Amaan, tel: (0)777 414 364/411 362. Well-named (House of Peace) hotel on the south side of Stone Town, opposite Victoria Gardens. Beautifully furnished, with original Zanzibari beds and large sitting room.
Chavda Hotel, tel: (0)24 223 2115. Converted Arab mansion, traditionally furnished. Rooftop bar and restaurant, good food. In Baghani.
Clove Hotel, tel: (0)777 484 567, email: clovehotel@ zanlink.com Clean and comfortable. Eight rooms and a spacious roof terrace where breakfast is served. Just behind House of Wonders.

Stone Town at a Glance

Dhow Palace, tel: (0)24 223 3012. Imaginatively converted old mansion in Baghani, with rooftop restaurant. Serves excellent spiced coffee and baked pastries for breakfast. Large rooms, good value for money, no alcohol.

Shangani Hotel, tel: (0)24 223 3688/6363, email: info@shanganihotel.com www.shanganihotel.com Attractive hotel opposite Old Post Office in most popular area of town. Twenty-eight spacious rooms, rooftop restaurant, coffee shop.

Zanzibar Palace, tel: (0)777 079 222, tel: (0)24 223 2230, tel: (0)733 079 222/047 370. Recently established old town house. Kiponda area of Stone Town.

LUXURY

Kisimani (Chavda Hotel), Baghani St, Baghani. International.

La Fenice, Shangani St, Shangani. Italian.

Le Spices Rendezvous (New Maharajah Rest), Kenyatta Rd, Vuga. Indian, including vegetarian, and international.

Sweet Eazy, Kenyatta Rd. Thai and African.

Tower Top Restaurant (236 Hurumzi), Hurumzi St. Open for dinner only and expensive but worth splashing out on as this place is well recommended. Various cuisines (menu changes daily). Very popular so book in advance.

Baharia (indoor) and **The Terrace** (on top) at Zanzibar Serena, Shangani Point. Basically French/international cuisine but with Swahili influences. Expensive but good.

MID-RANGE

Archipelago, Forodhani St. International/African.

Bahari (Tembo House), lovely location on seafront, international cuisine but no alcohol.

ETC Plaza, Suicide Alley/ Shangani St, Shangani. International/Swahili.

Mercury's, near Big Tree on waterfront, Mizingani Rd. Relaxed and popular restaurant and bar overlooking harbour, various types of food including good pizzas.

Monsoon, Forodhani Gardens. East Mediterranean/ international/Swahili. Popular, so book in advance.

Nyumbani, off Sokomuhogo St. Swahili.

Sambusa Two Tables, Victoria St just off Kaunda Rd, Vuga. Traditonal Zanzibari. Very good value.

Tradewinds (Africa House), Suicide Alley, Shangani. International/Swahili. Has recently been upgraded so might now be more expensive, but check.

The most popular excursions are the Spice Tours – among the best of which are those run by the Mitu family (*see* Tour Operators below) – or

trips to Jozani Forest to see the red colobus monkeys and/or Kizimkazi to see the dolphins (*see* references in appropriate chapters). Trips to beach resorts can also be arranged. Walking tours around Stone Town or boat trips around the harbour can be arranged. It is best to ask at your hotel or one of the tour operators (below) for current info.

Ferries: Azam Marine, tel: (0)24 223 1655; **Flying Horse**, tel: (0)24 223 3031; **Sea Express**, tel: (0)24 223 4690; **Sea Star**, tel: (0)24 223 4768. **Diving: Bahari Divers**, tel: (0)777 415 011; **One Ocean**, tel: (0)24 223 8374; **Scuba Do**, tel: (0)777 417 157.

Tour Operators: Blue Dolphin, east Changa Bazaar, tel: (0)777 424 858; **Eco+Culture Tours**, Hurumzi St, tel: (0)24 223 0366; tel: (0)777 410 873; **Gallery Tours and Safaris**, Kenyatta Road, tel: (0)24 223 2088; **Madeira Tours**, by Baghani Hotel, Baghani, tel: (0)24 223 0406; tel: (0)777 415 107; **Mitu's Spice Tours**, off Malawi Rd, Malindi, tel: (0)24 223 4636, tel: (0)777 418 098; **Sama Tours**, behind House of Wonders, tel: (0)24 223 3543; **Tabasam Tours**, Kenyatta Rd, tel: (0)24 223 0322; **Tropical Tours and Safaris**, Kenyatta Rd, tel: (0)777 413 454/411 121; **Zan Tours**, tel: (0)24 223 3116.

3
Around
Stone Town

NG'AMBO

Just across Creek Road from the Darajani district of Stone Town is Ali Hassan Mwinyi Road, alongside which are **more modern bazaars**, selling all kinds of goods, from electronic gadgets to hardware and perfumes, including *oud*, the traditional Omani perfume (*see* panel, page 7). The area, known as **Ng'ambo** (the Other Side, as it was on the far side of the original creek) is generally quite safe in the daytime but visitors should not walk around with valuables or large amounts of money.

THE OFFSHORE ISLETS

A very different experience is to take a boat ride (boats can be hired by the Big Tree or by the Tembo House Hotel among other places) to one or more of the offshore islets. Among the most popular is **Changuu**, formerly Prison Island, though the prison was only ever used as a quarantine station and is now a tourist lodge with restaurant. Changuu has a small, attractive beach and shallow lagoon suitable for snorkelling, plus a nature trail through its small forest where you might see tiny suni antelopes and various bird species. There is also, in an enclosure behind the restaurant, a colony of giant Aldabran tortoises, among them descendants of four originals presented to the British Regent in 1919.

Close to Changuu is **Chapwani**, formerly Grave Island, now privately owned and with its own small lodge and restaurant. British sailors who died of dis-

DON'T MISS

★★★ **Chumbe Island** (preferably snorkelling).
★★ **Changuu Island**.
★★ **Mbweni Ruins** and **Botanic Gardens**.
★★ **Princess Salme Tour**.
★ Visit to **Mtoni** and/or **Maruhubi Palace Ruins**.
★ Lunch at **Mangapwani** (book at the Sheraton) or fresh seafood at some good restaurant (like Mtoni Marine, for example).

Opposite: *A huge coconut crab on Chumbe Island. They can grow up to 1m (3ft) in size.*

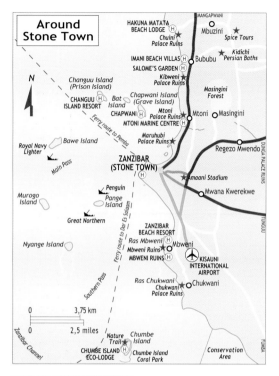

Around Stone Town

HAKUNA MATATA BEACH LODGE
MANGAPWANI
Chuini Palace Ruins
Mbuzini
Spice Tours
IMANI BEACH VILLAS
Bububu
Kidichi Persian Baths
SALOME'S GARDEN
N
Changuu Island (Prison Island)
Kibweni Palace Ruins
Masingini Forest
CHANGUU ISLAND RESORT
Bat Island
Chapwani Island (Grave Island)
CHAPWANI
Mtoni Palace Ruins
Mtoni
Masingini
MTONI MARINE CENTRE
Royal Navy Lighter
Bawe Island
Maruhubi Palace Ruins
Regezo Mwendo
ZANZIBAR (STONE TOWN)
Main Pass
Amaani Stadium
Penguin Island
Mwana Kwerekwe
Murogo Island
Pange Island
Great Northern
ZANZIBAR BEACH RESORT
Nyange Island
Ras Mbweni
Mbweni
Mbweni Ruins
MBWENI RUINS
KISAUNI INTERNATIONAL AIRPORT
Ras Chukwani
Chukwani
Chukwani Palace Ruins
0   3,75 km
0   2,5 miles
Nature Trail
Chumbe Island
CHUMBE ISLAND ECO-LODGE
Chumbe Island Coral Park
Conservation Area

ease or were killed on anti-slavery patrols, as well as those killed on *HMS Pegasus* when she was shelled by the German raider *Koenigsberg* in 1914, are buried on the island, hence its former English name. Chapwani has a fine beach and also good snorkelling, as well as a few interesting creatures such as dik-dik antelopes, fruit bats, coconut crabs and several bird species.

Not far away is **Bawe Island**, 6km (4 miles) west of Stone Town, uninhabited but popular with scuba divers. Some way to the south, however, about 6km (4 miles) southwest of Chukwani, is an even more inter-

esting islet, **Chumbe**. The **Chumbe Island Coral Park** is said to be one of the finest shallow-water reefs in the world. The associated lodge has won several awards for its outstanding contribution to conservation. It has no beach but as well as its fabulous coral gardens, which are wonderful for snorkellers, it has a fascinating nature trail through unspoilt coral rag forest. Among other creatures that can be found here are the reintroduced Ader's duiker, only found in Zanzibar and Kenya's Arabuko-Sokoke Forest, and the coconut crab (see panel, page 51).

Day trips to Chumbe can be arranged (a boat leaves the Mbweni Ruins Hotel, 7km/4.3 miles south of Stone Town, every morning at 10:00 but please check in advance).

THE COASTAL STRIP NORTH OF STONE TOWN
Livingstone House

One of the first buildings the traveller encounters when leaving Stone Town to head north is the double-storeyed **Livingstone House**, commissioned in Arab style by Sultan Majid. David Livingstone stayed here, courtesy of Majid, before his last fateful expedition, bemoaning 'the old, old way of living, eating, drinking, sleeping, sleeping, drinking, eating, slave dhows coming and slave dhows going away; and bad smells… it might be called Stinkibar rather than Zanzibar'. The house is opposite the old dhow harbour that extended, in those days, to the adjacent shore. It is now the headquarters of the Zanzibar Tourist Corporation.

Maruhubi Palace Ruins

A short distance further north are the **Maruhubi Palace Ruins**, down a leafy turn-off to the left. The palace was built by the enterprising Sultan Barghash in 1882 to house his 99 concubines and (rounding off his century) his one official wife. Guides on the spice tours, which often take in Maruhubi, sometimes tell tales of concubines being put to death if they did not satisfy their master, or after being lent out to visiting dignitaries, all of which is a load of nonsense.

None of his concubines satisfied him at Maruhubi itself, unless there were liaisons during its construction, as Barghash died before it was completed. Eleven years later it burned down, leaving little but the foundations of a bath house (from which the marble was stripped by thieves), some coral stone pillars that once supported the mostly wooden building, the remains of an aqueduct and some ornamental ponds. A sad end for a palace that was said to be Zanzibar's most charming, but there is a dreamy, intriguing poignancy about Maruhubi and it is pleasant to walk down its avenue of mangoes, imported from India, or to sit, as the women of the harem must have done, by the ponds, with their green carpets of lily pads and star-petalled flowers of cerulean blue.

COCONUT CRACKERS

Coconut crabs, unlike coconut macaroons, are the last thing you would want on your plate during afternoon tea at Chumbe Island Resort, as they can grow up to 1m (3ft) or more from leg tip to leg tip and weigh up to 4kg (9lb). Fortunately they are generally nocturnal and basically gentle creatures, though as well as eating coconuts (hence the name), other nuts, seeds and fleshy fruits, they will sometimes eat certain creatures, living or dead, such as other crabs. One was once observed catching and eating a Polynesian rat, though not, of course, on Zanzibar. The coconut crab (*Birgus latro*) climbs trees in search of coconuts (which it eats by cracking the nuts with its strong pincers to get at the flesh), to escape the heat or for security. It is the largest land-living arthropod in the world, and perhaps the world's most unusual thief – it is said that the crabs sometimes steal shiny items such as silverware (keep an eye on your cutlery). More certainly, they can live for 30 to 40 years, they mate frequently (if briefly), have an excellent sense of smell and despite being crabs cannot swim, except as larvae.

PALACE OF POIGNANT MEMORIES

No one should visit Mtoni Ruins without reading Princess Salme's memoirs (or alternatively taking the Princess Salme Tour from the nearby Mtoni Marine Centre). The sea has washed away much of the gardens where she passed idyllic childhood hours, and where peacocks, flamingoes, ostriches and gazelles wandered among exotic blossoming trees and shrubs. Here she would watch her beloved father, Said, sipping his coffee and admiring his fleet from the wooden pavilion (the Benjile) that overlooked the sea. *Taarab* concerts, with a traditional Zanzibar coffee ceremony, are now held in the courtyard.

Mtoni Palace Ruins

Another short distance to the north, down another turn-off to the left, is the oldest of Zanzibar's palaces, **Mtoni**. Once again, there isn't a great deal to see, though much to imagine, for this was Said the Great's first official residence in Zanzibar, built between 1828 and 1832. It was also the much-loved home of his daughter Salme, who recalled it in her memoirs years later, after eloping with and marrying the German merchant Heinrich Reute.

The palace once bustled with activity (its population sometimes numbered about 1000, including Said's three official wives, 75 concubines, countless children and grandchildren, servants and slaves) and was lavishly furnished. It is now reduced to walls. The ***Beit el-Ras***, a little further north, was built by Said to accommodate Mtoni's overflow, but is in even greater ruin, only its giant porch, high adjacent arches and some steps remaining in the grounds of what is now a teacher training college.

Even more than Maruhubi, Mtoni's ruins are rich in atmosphere for anyone familiar with their background. Sadly, Princess Salme's favourite part of the complex, the Benjile, is no longer in evidence. It was a strange wooden structure, like a bandstand with a conical roof, overlooking the sea, where Said would proudly pace around sipping coffee and admiring his fleet, watched by his adoring daughter. Important conservation work is presently going on at the site; hopefully the Benjile, and the palace itself, will be restored or, where necessary, re-created.

Below: *One of several palatial ruins along the coast close to Stone Town.*

Kibweni Palace

One palace follows another; next in line is **Kibweni**, still less than 10km (6 miles) from Stone Town. Standing above the beach atop a steep sea wall, Kibweni was a most attractive country palace where the sultan and his family and friends could relax; in fact, Kibweni, when it was built in 1915 (in Arab style but by the British authorities), was named *Beit el-Kassrusaada*, Palace of Happiness. Sultan Khalifa bin Harub, who reigned from 1911–60, used it as an out-of-town residence and it now serves a similar purpose for Zanzibar's less aristocratic ruling elite.

Bububu

Just north of Kibweni is the high-density town of **Bububu**, its onomatopoeic name derived from the bubbling spring that was situated nearby or from the whistle of the engine on the Bububu Railway (*see* panel, this page).

Bububu has two good hotels, **Salome's Garden** and the **Imani Beach Villas**, plus the still-popular **Fuji Beach Bar**, once owned by a Japanese gentleman (the entire Bububu strand became known as Fuji Beach). The beach would be highly regarded in most countries but by Zanzibar's exalted standards is quite ordinary. The two hotels and bar, however, make it well worth considering, especially Salome's Garden, which has historic connections, the original building having been built by Sultan Said and occupied, so it is said, by his 'wayward' daughter Salme just prior to her elopement.

Chuini Palace Ruins

Less than 3km (2 miles) north of Bububu, down yet another left-hand turn-off, are the ruins of **Chuini Palace**, another example of Barghash's near-obsession with regal buildings and the latest technology, for Chuini was built (in 1872) above the bed of a stream, to provide running water in the days before electricity. Sultan Ali bin Said added to it but Chuini (Place of the Leopard) burned down in 1914, despite the flowing water. All very academic, as you cannot visit it anyway.

THE BUBUBU RAILWAY

This unlikely feat of engineering, the first railway in Africa, stretched from Bububu to the sultan's summer palace at Chukwani, south of Stone Town. The sultan in question, needless to say, was the irrepressibly entrepreneurial Barghash. Sadly, the little-used railway was dismantled after his death but a second line was established by an American company in the early years of the 20th century, between Bububu and the Old Fort in Stone Town (the entrance gate was removed to allow the train to enter). Henry Ford, indirectly, ended the railway's adventures by inventing the motor car, and by 1927 the track was derelict.

WORKING GIRLS

The Mbweni Ruins include the Industrial Wing, where less academic ex-slave girls once laundered the delicate bits and pieces that normally adorned Zanzibar's more exalted ladies, and were taught embroidery and patchwork quilting. They also plaited traditional mats from dyed palm fronds, which were used as seats, curtains and sheets for the living and as palls to wrap the uncoffined dead. Not much fun, but better than the horrors and humiliations of slavery.

CHUKWANI PALACE

About two kilometres south of Mbweni, by the sea, is all that remains (the bath house) of another of Barghash's palaces, Chukwani, used as a kind of health spa until it was demolished. The site cannot be visited.

THE COASTAL STRIP SOUTH OF STONE TOWN
Mbweni

Just 7km (4 miles) south of Stone Town, on a blunt promontory, is the pleasant suburb of Mbweni. Its main attraction for tourists are the **Mbweni Ruins** and the hotel named after them. The ruins are the remnants of a 19th-century Anglican mission, set up in the early 1870s under Bishop Steere to house, educate and train girls who had been freed from the horrors of the slave dhows, or who were the daughters of freed slaves. They are surrounded by a wonderful botanic garden lovingly established by an English artist, Flo Liebst, and are very atmospheric, especially as the sun sets beyond the adjacent sea.

John Kirk's House

Many of the plants in Flo's garden were taken from **John Kirk's House** nearby, purpose-built by Sultan Barghash for his close friend and advisor, the British consul. Just south of Mbweni witchcraft, never far away in Africa, was said to flourish, with intriguingly unspecified 'rites often being performed on the beach', but Kirk reserved his own kind of magic for diplomacy and horticulture. He established an experimental garden at Mbweni, at his own expense, most of the plants coming from Kew in London. The plants included aloes, tea, coffee, cacao, mahogany, orchids, rubber trees, vanilla and palms.

His tall old house, which stands on private land owned by members of the powerful Karume family, has been allowed to fall into near-collapse (again one wonders why) but is still surrounded by some of his original plants or their descendants, now untended. Kirk later sold the house to Caroline Thackeray, cousin of the celebrated English essayist and novelist and teacher at the Mbweni school for freed slave girls. Miss Thackeray lived there until her death in 1926. She is buried in the graveyard of **St John's Church** a little distance away. The lovely old church looks like a lost and lonely English expatriate among the tropical greenery, though on closer inspection it has some distinctly Eastern features, not least a fine doorway.

Around Stone Town at a Glance

As for Stone Town.

Most people use **taxis** (haggle beforehand, not afterwards). A cheaper alternative is to catch a *dala-dala* (local mini-bus) though these can be crowded, and only operate during day-light hours. *Dala-dalas* (and their drivers) are a law unto themselves but there is a kind of order in the 'functional anarchy'; each is assigned to a particular route (announced by signs on the *dala-dalas* themselves) so make sure you get the right one. They stop more or less anywhere but there are regular 'stands', one of the main ones being at Darajani, opposite the market complex on Creek Road. Ask at your hotel.

North of Stone Town
LUXURY
Hakuna Matata Beach Lodge, tel: (0)777 454 892, email: info@zanzibar-resort.com www.hakuna-matata-beach-lodge.com Luxury bungalows just beyond Bububu, on privately owned bay, among ruins of Chuini Palace. Planetarium coming soon.

MID-RANGE
Imani Beach Villas, tel: (0)24 225 0050, www.imani.it Off the main road in Bububu, just inland of Fuji Beach. Small, Italian-run resort among gar-

dens, restaurant serves good seafood. Various excursions.
Salome's Garden, tel: (0)24 225 0050. Opposite Imani Beach Villas just off the main road in Bububu (inland of Fuji Beach), amid gardens, orchard and ruins. Very atmospheric.
Mtoni Marine Centre, tel: (0)24 225 0140, www.mtoni.com Popular and friendly resort, set among palm groves and lawns along-side the sea and close to the ruins of Mtoni Palace. Caters for all budgets. Swimming pool and children's play-ground. Good restaurants.

South of Stone Town
LUXURY
Mbweni Ruins Hotel, tel: (0)24 223 5478/9, email: hotel@mbweni.com www.mbweni.com Lovely hotel 20 minutes south of Stone Town, set among enchanting botanic gardens, alongside 19-century ruins. Pleasant little beach, swimming pool, good restau-rant with views.

Offshore Islets
LUXURY
Bawe Tropical Island, tel: (0)786 301 662/3, reserva-tions (0)272 544 595, (0)754 254 602, email: info.bawe@privateislands-zanzibar.com www.privateislands-zanzibar.com Fifteen de luxe, sea-facing cottages, swimming pool, restaurant and bar on little private island just west of Stone Town.

Changuu Private Island Paradise, tel: (0)786 301 662/3, reservations (0)272 544 595, (0)754 254 602, email: info.changuu@privateislands-zanzibar.com www.private islands-zanzibar.com Originally built as a prison in the 19th century, now a place (according to the ads) 'where you would want to spend a life sentence'. Exterior still fairly forbidding but don't let this put you off as there are four bars, a floodlit tennis court and swim-ming pool, plus a little private island, a beach to lounge around on and a little coral reef for snorkelling. A short boat ride from Stone Town.
Chumbe Island Eco-Lodge, tel: (0)24 223 1040, tel: (0)777 413 582, www.chumbeisland.com Seven rustic, split-level *bandas* in this magnificent eco-sensitive lodge, noted for its location by one of the world's finest shallow water coral reefs, off Mbweni. Not cheap but worth paying for at least once. Transfer by boat from Mbweni Ruins Hotel included in the cost.

Most people eat at their hotel or (if day trippers) back in Stone Town.

As for Stone Town.

As for Stone Town.

4
Northern Unguja

Unguja, north of the road that leads from Stone Town
to Chwaka on the east coast, is extremely fertile in its
western two-thirds. This is where Unguja's clove plantations are established, as well as sugar-cane fields, rice
paddies, groves of coconuts and the island's celebrated
spice gardens. Its more arid eastern sector is composed of
coral rag, with its associated scrub and scatterings of larger
trees. Its beaches are superb. There are a few smaller ones
along the west coast but the best are to be found around
the northern headland, at Kendwa and Nungwi, and along
the eastern coast down to Chwaka Bay. Here and there are
some interesting ruins.

THE SPICE TOURS
No one should leave Unguja without embarking on a
spice tour, preferably one with an alfresco lunch included,
such as those organized by the Mitu family. Mzee (Old Man)
Mitu, a one-time taxi driver who initiated the tours, is now
retired but his sons have inherited their father's hard-won
knowledge and know how to impart it in a most absorb-
ing, good-natured way.

The tours leave after breakfast (the latest around 09:30)
and return, if lunch is included, after a wonderful meal,
usually of pilau rice with locally grown vegetables and of
course many of the spices you will have just seen growing.
Lunch is cooked by village women and often taken seated on
mats (as the sultans traditionally ate) in an open-sided *banda*
(thatched hut). On the way out you will probably stop briefly
by Livingstone's House and at some stage at Maruhubi Ruins

DON'T MISS

★★★ **Mnemba Island:** staying
at the exclusive lodge if you
can afford it, diving or
snorkelling around the atoll
if you can't!
★★★ At least two nights in a
good **beach resort** (Nungwi
if you are young or young at
heart, with perhaps a moon-
rave thrown in).
★★★ **Spice Tour** (with lunch).
★ **Turtle Aquarium**, Nungwi.
★ Watching **dhow-building**,
Nungwi.
★ **Seafood** in a good restaurant
(lobster if you can afford it).

Opposite: *Colourful
aromatic spices for sale.*

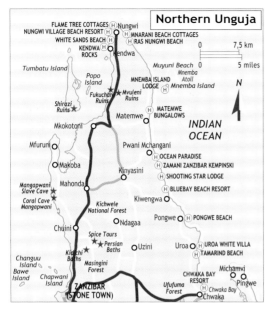

Northern Unguja

and the **Kidichi Baths**. The baths were once part of a palace built by Said for his second wife, Binte Irich Mirza, the granddaughter of the Shah of Persia and sometimes known as Sheherazade. They are well preserved and embellished with stucco decorations depicting peacocks, palm trees, lotus flowers and (appropriately) cloves, the work of Persian Zoroastrians as the Qur'an discourages Muslims from depicting Allah or his creations.

Another place you might visit, probably after the spice tour itself, is **Mangapwani**, 20km (12 miles) or so north of Stone Town on the coast. There is a pleasant beach here, where the Serena Hotel puts on lunches if you book in advance, and two caves. One, the **Coral Cave**, is by the beach itself, the second, known as the **Slave Cave** (or Chamber), is just north of the beach. Guides will sometimes tell you that slaves were once kept in the Coral Cave but this is probably untrue. The cave is interesting, however, as it is one of many places in Zanzibar (and Tanzania) that has spiritual associations; locals come here to leave simple offerings for the spirits, to bring good luck or blessings, in a semi-animistic departure from their mainstream Islam beliefs. They also come to draw cool, fresh water from the pool within the cave.

The more northerly cave, however, was adapted as a holding place for slaves and still has an atmosphere of quiet foreboding. There is a narrow tunnel in its gloomy depths, which could be sealed by a wooden door. The tunnel leads to two **chambers** hewn from the coral, where slaves would be kept out of sight of any naval anti-slaving

---

PORRIDGE AND PERFUMED PETALS...

Zanzibari men are said to stir nutmeg into their wives' or girlfriends' porridge 'to make the women say (and presumably do) nice things', and jasmine is sometimes scattered on the beds of brides to 'excite them' (though the Arabs thought it depressed the male libido, which seems to defeat the object). One needs to be aware of these things, as jasmine is sometimes laid on the pillows of Zanzibar's hotel guests, and Zanzibari beds are quite romantic to start with...

patrols until it was safe for them to be shipped out, by night and in deplorable conditions, to the Gulf and elsewhere.

The spice farms themselves begin only a little way from Stone Town, the journey taking you through typically lush western Unguja country of sugar and spice and all things nice, including groves of coconut and attractive little villages among their clumps of mango and bananas. Many huts are now built of cement blocks, with corrugated-iron roofs, though you can still see more traditional huts of mud and wattle, with roofs of *makuti* (palm thatch).

You will witness, in passing, brief cameos of Swahili village life, some unchanged for centuries; women pounding maize or fetching water, sometimes in a tin *debe* or these days a colourful plastic bucket, men or women working in the *shambas* (small farms) or sitting chatting with friends and neighbours on the *baraza* of their modest homes. Children might be playing football or piloting cars, made from wood with an attached stick, along the roadside. Cyclists saunter by on their Chinese 'Flying Pigeons', ox carts (rarely seen on the mainland) jog by and the island's country buses rumble past, their wooden coachwork and slatted seats recalling the railway carriages once hauled by Stephenson's *Rocket*. In the leafy shade or in the dust, goats might be browsing, cows chewing the cud, chickens scratching or squabbling.

You will sometimes see, amidst the luxuriant greenery, the blue-grey smoke from coconut drying kilns. The nuts are harvested four times a year by pickers who climb the lofty trees assisted by a thong tied between the feet. The outer husks of the nuts are later removed by impaling the nuts on a sharp metal spike. The exposed inner shell is then split in half and partially dried to enable the kernel to be removed, after which the kernel is dried for several more days, becoming copra (*see* panel, this page).

The spice farms are situated among these villages and their surrounding greenery. The clove is still king, though production and prices have fallen dramatically over recent decades. Zanzibar has been forced to diversify, as you will discover as you are led from one part of the spice gardens to the next, to see, touch, smell and

SWISS ARMY KNIFE OF A TREE

Copra, the dried kernel of the coconut, is turned into coconut oil, used in the manufacture of soap, candles, margarine and hair and skin oils. The residue goes into making cattle feed and the fibre of the coconut (coir) into the production of ropes, matting, brooms and mattresses. The coconut palm also provides a beautifully dark-flecked timber used for furniture, as well as roofing thatch, fuel, spoons, water ladles, fish traps and nets. Truly a multipurpose tree.

FORBIDDEN FRUIT

The durian originated in Borneo and many people think it should have stayed there. The fruit is actually banned in certain places but its admirers call it 'the king of fruits'. Its smell has been compared to garlic, rotting meat, sewage and sweaty socks, yet a famous 19th-century naturalist compared its taste to: 'A rich, butter-like custard highly flavoured with almonds…intermingled with wafts of flavour that call to mind cream cheese, onion sauce, brown sherry and other incongruities.' Maybe his sinuses were blocked…

Above: *A traditional basket weaver at work.*

eventually taste a sensual inventory of spices, including nutmeg (and its lacy red covering, mace), cinnamon, cardamom, peppermint, lemon grass, vanilla, turmeric, ginger, chilli, pepper and betel nut, as well as other plants such as the lipstick tree or perhaps jasmine.

Anyone not already seduced by spices will surely succumb to the fruits that you will also encounter, from bananas, oranges, grapefruit, limes, mangoes, pomegranates, mulberries, lychees, guavas and avocados to the even more exotic (for Western visitors at least) paw-paw, breadfruit, jackfruit, rambutan, Malay apple, sapodilla, pomelo, Indian plum, soursop, star apple, rose apple, durian (that 'smells like hell and tastes like heaven') and mangosteen.

Having feasted your eyes (and mind) on this cornucopia you will then, assuming lunch is included, get the chance to feast on some of them more literally. You will also get the opportunity to buy spices, often attractively packaged, from some little village stall, so that, like Princess Salme with her little bag of Mtoni sand, you can take a token of Zanzibar with you when you leave.

FOREST FRAGMENTS

Much of northern Unguja's natural moist forest has gone but there are two important exceptions. Beyond the Dunga Ruins, 4km (2.5 miles) or so west of Chwaka, is **Ufufuma Forest**, little known to tourists but worth a visit for anyone interested in wildlife or in the preservation of Zanzibar's fast-diminishing natural forests. Ufufuma is locally (and enthusiastically) managed, and as well as a small group of Zanzibar red colobus monkeys there are also duikers and dik-diks, some introduced impalas and some interesting bird species.

Kichwele National Forest is just to the northeast of the main spice tour destinations and is largely planted with rubber, though a small area of natural forest survives, and

---

SPICE UP YOUR EDUCATION

Spice tours educate the mind, not merely the senses. You learn that black, red and white peppers come from the same plant; that vanilla pods contain 35 other sweet-smelling substances; that liquorice also comes from the pod of a tree; that all parts of the ginger tree, not only its roots, are aromatic, and that the tree's resin is used to make lacquers, varnishes and incense; and that nutmeg, rumoured to be capable of sending women wild, is also used, appropriately enough, to make perfumes.

like Ufufuma is home to a number of translocated red colobus monkeys, some small antelopes and various birds. Hopefully the forest will soon be transformed into something more extensive and more typical of its original state, with nature trails and tourist facilities.

THE BEACHES
The beaches of northern Unguja are among the best in Zanzibar. They (and their attendant resorts) all have their individual character, and are therefore listed separately here:

Nungwi and Kendwa
The road from Stone Town to Nungwi takes the traveller through the green luxuriance typical of northwest Unguja, characterized by coconut, sugar and clove plantations with villages here and there among clusters of bananas and mangoes. At one point it passes through the fishing village of **Mkokotoni**, its boats lying languidly at anchor on a beautiful blue sea with **Tumbatu Island** less than 3km (2 miles) away across the straits. Soon afterwards the lush cultivation phases erratically into coral rag country, its largely evergreen bush and dry scrub relieved by occasional mature trees, including baobabs.

Nungwi itself is a fishing village at the extreme northern tip of Unguja, with a functional charm and a friendly and tolerant population. It also boasts a dhow-building centre, a lighthouse, a natural aquarium and two small supermarkets. A **cultural tour** of Nungwi can be booked at the aquarium. It consists of a two-and-a-half-hour stroll around the village to see old mosques, markets, basket-weaving, trees and plants of medicinal value, and a 'haunted' salt-water well.

The lighthouse is out of bounds and photography discouraged, no great loss as unlike its ancient Alexandrian counterpart it is not one of the world's wonders. The adjacent aquarium, part of a natural tidal basin, is more interesting. It is home to several green and a smaller number of hawksbill turtles. The green turtles are quite large and tame; you can hand-feed them with seaweed or even swim among them, though the water is a bit soupy. The

---

FUKUCHANI RUINS

In terms of historic buildings (other than those mentioned in the previous chapter) northern Zanzibar has little to offer except the Fukuchani Ruins. They are often known locally (and probably erroneously) as the Portuguese House but archaeologists believe them to be Swahili in origin. They are situated just over 10km (6 miles) south of Nungwi, just beyond Fukuchani Village to the west of the main Stone Town–Nungwi Road. Apparently dating back to the 16th century, they are not dramatically exciting, but the thick-walled remains of a coral ragstone house are in good condition. Slits in the stonework are thought to have served as openings for firearms, perhaps against the possibility of threats from the marauding Portuguese. People travelling to or from Nungwi independently might want to stop off there; more energetic holiday-makers might want to cycle there and back from Nungwi.

REPTILES OF THE REEF

Five species of turtle have been recorded around Zanzibar but the most common are the green (*Chelonia mydas*) and the hawksbill (*Eretmochelys imbricata*). The green can grow to 1.5m (5ft) long and lives almost entirely (as an adult) on sea grass and seaweed. Where unmolested (sadly a rare situation nowadays) it will often come out on to beaches to bask. The smaller (up to 1m/3.3ft) hawksbill, though omnivorous, lives mainly on sea sponges.

NO CHAMPAGNE SEND-OFF

The dhow-builders of Nungwi, like many seafarers, are God-fearing and superstitious. As specific stages of the craft are reached, little ceremonies are held, sometimes involving the sacrifice of a goat and a reading from the Qur'an. On the boat's completion a larger ceremony takes place, attended by many villagers. In many shipyards, a bottle of champagne is broken on the ship's bows at the naming and launching ceremony; in Islamic Nungwi the builder is content to hammer on his creation three times.

hawksbills seem more reclusive. On your way to or from the aquarium you might spend some time watching craftsmen building dhows along the adjacent beach, using tools and techniques that have hardly changed in centuries.

It is their first glance of the sea, however, that stops many first-time visitors to Nungwi in their tracks, as they realize that the photographs in the brochures and on the websites, showing blindingly white sands and turquoise waters, were not computer-enhanced after all. On the northwest corner of the headland, several resorts lie side by side, a short way back from a low sea wall, which also acts as a catwalk for an irregular procession of passers-by, tourists and locals, providing some interesting people-watching.

The sea provides its own distracting *passeggiata*, with incoming or outgoing dhows, when the tide is in, sails mostly as white as Nungwi's sands against the luminous sea, and when the tide is out scores of local people, mostly women, scouring the rock pools for anything edible. Opposite Nungwi Village, just to the east, the *mashua* at evening and sunrise lie 'idle as painted ships upon a painted ocean', their raked masts forming a forest, whilst in the opposite direction the sunsets can be blissfully serene.

A short walk to the southwest of this sea wall strip brings you to a more crowded, more lively cluster of resorts, restaurants and bars, some little more than Rastafarian-owned shacks that seem to be held together by friction, others miniature villages on timber piles, perched above the aptly named Paradise Beach and looking out upon picture-postcard seas or shelves of seaweed-strewn coral, depending on the tide.

The Zanzibari Rastas (*see* panel, page 64) take many visitors by surprise; how authentically Rastafari they are is a question only they can answer, but they look convincing, with their dreadlocks and sometimes their capacious, colourful Rasta caps. Their lifestyle also seems to emulate that of their Jamaican brothers-in-belief; some of the Rastas, mellowed by marijuana (*ganja*) and/or the odd bottle of lager, sometimes seem to be in a state of suspended animation. They tend to come alive, in their slow, rhythmic way, at sundown, especially in peak season and around the nights of the full moon, when moon-rave parties, with reggae and rock, enliven (or desecrate, depending on your point of view) this western sector of the Nungwi coast.

Just beyond the main cluster of restaurants, bars, hotels and dive centres that perch on the low cliffs and timber decks in this area is a little avenue of kiosks selling colourfully naive *tinga-tinga* **paintings**. The best are genuine works of art, the worst not worth the cost of the board they are painted on, but in between is a range of themes that, however corny or derivative, have their appeal. Collectively, in this little lane with its line of paw-paw trees, the pictures' uninhibited reds and yellows provide a cheerful foreground to the equally unlikely blues of the sea. And as one of the artists claims to be Vincent van Gogh, you might just pick up something that will change your life forever.

A few kilometres further south is **Kendwa**, with its own burgeoning line of resorts and beautiful beach, as happy a marriage of land and sea as anyone might wish for. The beach is broader than that further north but like Nungwi's it has much less of a tidal range than the east coast beaches, making it accessible for swimming for much longer periods. The resorts, on the whole, are thankfully in keeping with Zanzibar's private, unobtrusive nature, though things are changing. The sprawling package tourist resorts have begun to move in, and the moon-raves are already popular, but for now Kendwa is relatively unspoilt.

East of Nungwi's lighthouse the shoreline falls away sharply to the south. In this vicinity, still within walking distance of the village, are several more resorts, including more up-market ones. They are less numerous and crowded than those further west, and more appealing to those who enjoy seclusion and silence. The beaches here

TINGA-TINGA

Tinga-tinga painting is named after Eduardo Tinga Tinga, of the Makonde people, who settled in Dar es Salaam and realized, in the 1960s, that he could make a meagre living from his work. This involved painting, with bicycle paint, on masonite boards (and nowadays on just about anything else). The thick, often brightly coloured paint, characteristically covering every square centimetre of space, gives *tinga-tinga* paintings their vibrancy, immediacy and clarity of form. Sadly, Eduardo was eventually mistaken for a thief by police and shot dead.

Below: *Colourful* tinga-tinga *paintings are not everyone's cup of tea, but some can be quite beautiful.*

tend to be broader and at least as attractive as those west
of the lighthouse, but with a much greater tidal range,
which often limits swimming to six-hours-or-so 'windows
of opportunity'. From November to January, when the
northeast trades are blowing, they can be littered with seaweed; we are talking, after all, about the sea…

Muyuni Beach

Eleven or 12km (7/7.5 miles) southeast of Nungwi Village
is the first of a long, scarcely broken line of splendid
beaches (and a whole beaded necklace of resorts, the
good, the bad and the ugly) that make up Unguja's
Sunrise Coast. Until recently the 2–3km (1–2-mile) long
Muyuni Beach had escaped the attentions of the developers but this is about to change; a 76ha (188-acre) plot
(the size of a modest farm) has been marked out and by
2009 will become the latest of Unguja's large resorts
(with a 50-room residence and spa retreat and a 150-
room luxury hotel).

Mnemba Island

However exclusive the new hotel at Muyuni might be, it
will not be as exclusive as **Mnemba Island** just 3km (2
miles) offshore. Mnemba is often described, predictably,
as 'the jewel in Unguja's crown' and, with its emerald (or
at least vibrant green) vegetation set off by near-white

Below: *The beaches of
Matemwe are less private
than those at Mnemba
Island, but no less
beautiful.*

sands against a turquoise
and ultramarine sea, it
isn't hard to see why. As
with most jewels, it is
privately owned and
doesn't come cheap
(among the clients at the
Mnemba Island Lodge
were Bill Gates and
Naomi Campbell; not as a
twosome, needless to say).
Anyone attempting to land
there without a prior
booking will be encour-

aged to depart, hopefully politely. Don't despair; the rest of the coral atoll is accessible even to the low-budget brigade, providing superb snorkelling and diving. If you want to goggle at Microsoft CEOs or rub wet suits with supermodels, this might be your moment.

Matemwe Beach

Mnemba's beaches are more private though no better than those at **Matemwe**, a short distance to the southwest on the main coast. And Matemwe, with its little fishing village and small number of resorts set along the palm-fringed beaches or on one of the coral outcrops that occasionally break the continuity of powdery white sand, is an intimate place, popular with expatriates long before Unguja was discovered by everyone else. Nevertheless its closeness to Mnemba Island, for snorkellers or divers, is one of its greatest assets.

Pwani Mchangani

This Coast of Sand is aptly named, and happily the small village with its fine beach (a southern extension of that at Matemwe) has not quite surrendered to the more insensitive developers. It is fighting a losing battle, however, as the besieging armies set up their pavilions of splendour just to the south.

Kiwengwa

Kiwengwa Beach, similar to that at Pwani Mchangani, has fallen to the invaders. The village itself is some 11km (7 miles) south of Pwani, seemingly keeping its distance (but only just) from the super-resorts to the north. These are dominated by great, all-under-one-roof enclaves, the playgrounds of the package tourists, mostly Italians. It is tempting to lambaste or patronize package tourism but it provides enjoyment and entertainment for a large number of often decent, hard-working people. But the question cannot be avoided: why spend hard-earned money to fly to Zanzibar to do what you could do (more or less) back in Italy when Zanzibar, so fascinating, is on the other side of the walls?

PAMPERING TO OUR EVERY NEED...

If you are privileged enough to stay at Mnemba Island Lodge your every need (give or take a few) will be taken care of, but for the rest of us, even those who stay in tiny Rasta shacks, there is hope at hand. Many resorts around Unguja now have spas, and most have either resident or itinerant professional pamperers, eager (at least if you are female) to braid your hair into wonderful African-type creations or to trace beautifully intricate patterns on your hands or feet with henna, a practice originally reserved for Southeast Asian brides, and for other women attending the wedding (or any other celebratory occasion). You can also have a massage (the men can join in here) or pedicure right there on the beach, with the soporific sound of the surf in the background. If you don't feel relaxed after all that, perhaps you need to cut down on the caffeine – not easy in Zanzibar where the coffee can be superb.

Above: *Fishermen with their fishing nets.*

Pongwe

The question might also be asked, why all these developments north of Kiwengwa Village when the beaches by **Pongwe** Village, only 5km (3 miles) to the south, are so delightful and so relatively *unde*veloped? The beaches take the form of sequestered clear-water coves between outcrops of coral, their sands as close to white as makes no difference and almost as predictably enhanced by palms; another candidate (and a convincing one) for the best beach in Zanzibar.

Uroa and Chwaka

Last in this long line of Unguja's northeastern beaches is **Uroa**, alongside the rather rambling and unprepossessing village of that name, at the northwestern corner of Chwaka Bay. Like most other east coast beaches it is composed of fine coral sand backed by palms or casuarinas, shelving into a shallow lagoon that at low tide becomes a bare expanse of coral shelf, dimpled with rock pools and combed by the locals for edible creatures and seaweed. Its beach never seems to vie for the best-in-Zanzibar title and it can be a bit dreary when skies are grey and a stiff monsoon is blowing, but so can anywhere else and most countries in the world would be glad to have it.

Eight kilometres (5 miles) to the south is **Chwaka Village**, generally bypassed by tourists, though the sunrises across Chwaka Bay can be photogenic and the bay itself, half-girdled by mangroves, can provide keen birders with a few worthwhile sightings. An open-air market is held on the shore and the fishermen, as they sail in with their catch or spend their shore leave mending nets or fashioning fish traps and lobster pots, provide other fairly interesting distractions.

CATCH AS CATCH CAN

Fishing along the East African coast has evolved into a multiplicity of methods, depending on the habits and preferred habitats of the fish sought. Two kinds of gill netting are practised, allowing fish of a certain size to push their heads through the mesh but not their bodies, thus ensnaring them by their gills when they try to back out. Other methods include trolling (using one or more baited lines from a moving boat), long-lining (using long lines with many short lines attached at intervals), hand-lining and (at night when lights are used to attract the shoals) seine netting, in which long, 'tennis court' type nets that hang down from the surface are used. In suitable areas some seine netting is carried out on foot, from the shallows. Trapping is also employed, using wicker or wire traps.

Northern Unguja at a Glance

BEST TIMES TO VISIT

Mid-May to mid-October, when temperatures and humidity are lowest and rainfall usually minimal, though all other times of year outside the long rains (approx. mid-March to mid-May) can be enjoyable. Mid-October to mid-March can sometimes be uncomfortably hot and humid, sometimes with showers, but off-sea breezes help to counteract this and diving is at its best during this period. Some beaches in the north and northeast can get strewn with seaweed in January and February but are otherwise superb.

GETTING THERE

Taxis are frequently used (haggle beforehand) but a cheaper alternative is to take a **'tourist' mini-bus** from outside the Old Fort in Stone Town or wherever else (ask at your hotel but shop around if you have the time and patience). Such mini-buses are usually clean, comfortable and efficient though you will usually have to share them (hence the lower costs) and they might not always leave on time (they tend to have at least two departure times but do not operate after about 13:00 or 14:00). Zanzibaris usually get around by *dala-dala* (*see* Around Stone Town at a Glance). The traditional ones are wooden-framed buses, from which

you emerge with a wooden-framed bottom, the modern ones less 'charming' but more comfortable. Both tend to be crowded.

GETTING AROUND

Most people tend to stay within walking distance of their resorts or hire bicycles, though taxis are often available. Boats are of course provided by resorts, water-sports centres, etc. for scuba-diving/ snorkelling enthusiasts or for trips to outlying islets.

WHERE TO STAY

Kendwa
MID-RANGE TO BUDGET
Kendwa Rocks, tel: (0)777 415 527, www. kendwarocks.com Rastafarian-run hotel with the laid-back informality that this might imply, including moon-raves (full-moon beach parties). Various types of accommodation including huts on stilts and brick-built bungalows. Popular with the younger set and for many people perhaps the best of Kendwa's options.
White Sands Beach Hotel, tel: (0)777 480 987, www.zanzibar-white-sands-hotel.com Unassuming but pleasant enough, with three kinds of rooms on the low coral cliffs alongside the beach, the best in two bungalows overlooking the sea. Well-designed restaurant and bar.

Nungwi
LUXURY
Mnarani Beach Cottages, tel: (0)24 224 0494, www. mnaranibeach.com Intimate, friendly little resort just east of Nungwi Village. Either small, individual cottages or family-size two-storey apartments.
Ras Nungwi Beach Hotel, tel: (0)24 223 3767/2512, www. rasnungwi.com Peaceful, colonial-style hotel about 3km (2 miles) from Nungwi Village, on northeastern tip of headland and on beautiful beach. Among Nungwi's best resorts, with 32 rooms, all with a/c, balconies. Swimming pool and dive centre.

MID-RANGE
Flame Tree Cottages, tel: (0)777 479 429, (0)786 350 828, email: etgl@zanlink.com www.flametreecottages.com Quietly pleasant, well-run hotel with clean and comfortable bungalows set around attractive gardens. Good shore-side location close to Nungwi Village. Motorized dhow available for snorkelling trips to Mnemba, etc. Good value for money.
Nungwi Village Beach Resort, tel: (0)22 215 2187, www.nungwivillage.com Pleasant place in good location on northern headland, close to Nungwi Village. Rooms with sea views or cheaper rooms around a courtyard further back. Mid-range and slightly below.

Northern Unguja at a Glance

Matemwe
LUXURY

Matemwe Bungalows, tel: (0)777 425 788. Long-time favourite with Tanzania's expat community, this simple, homely resort has moved more up-market. Perched along low coral cliffs just southwest of Mnemba atoll with its superb diving and snorkelling opportunities, the 14 bungalows each have a verandah overlooking the superb shoreline. Good wholesome food.

Mnemba Island Lodge, tel: (0)24 223 3110, email: mnemba@zitec.org www.mnemba-island.com Situated on a private island just northeast of Matemwe. Advertised as 'offering privacy and rustic exclusivity' (in '10 romantic beachside *bandas* [huts]') – and much else. At a price. But the location is idyllic and very exclusive and the service as good as you would expect.

Kiwengwa/Pwani Mchangani
LUXURY

Bluebay Beach Resort, tel: (0)24 224 0241/2/3/4, email: reservations@bluebay zanzibar.com One of the walled super-resorts that have homed in on this stretch of beach (which is well worth homing in on) but with more eco-awareness than most. Lots of amenities and activities, good diving/snorkelling centre.

Ocean Paradise, tel: (0)777 440 0990/1/2/3/4/5, email: info@oceanparadise zanzibar.com www.ocean paradisezanzibar.com Large Arabian-owned resort amid landscaped gardens. One of the better, more stylish super-resorts in this vicinity. Huge swimming pool, many water sports and other facilities.

Zamani Zanzibar Kempinski, central reservations tel: (0)744 444 477, email: reservations.Zanzibar@ kempinski.com www. kempinski.com Large, walled-in but well-appointed five-star beach hotel on the Kiwengwa/Pwani coastline.

MID-RANGE

Shooting Star Lodge, tel: (0)777 414 166. On a low cliff offering wonderful views to seaward. A refreshing, stylish alternative to the large resorts, with the intimacy and authenticity that they often lack. Small infinity pool and (reputedly) one of Zanzibar's best restaurants.

Pongwe
MID-RANGE

Pongwe Beach Hotel, tel: (0)777 413 973, www. pongwe.com Security said to be tight (with regard to casual callers) but once inside the hotel is very pleasant and the beach magnificent, as is the cuisine. Thirteen or so thatched bungalows in extensive, mature gardens.

Uroa
MID-RANGE

Tamarind Beach Hotel, tel: (0)24 223 7154, tel: (0)777 411 191, www.tamarind hotelzanzibar.com Friendly, easy-going place with about 14 clean and comfortable rooms in attractive, semi-detached cottages. Just north of Chwaka.

Uroa White Villa, tel: (0)741 326 874, www. uroawhitevilla.net German-run resort on the beach by Uroa Village. Clean, comfortable accommodation, good Swahili-style food.

Chwaka
MID-RANGE

Chwaka Bay Resort, tel: (0)24 224 0289. Situated on a fine beach by Chwaka Bay marine sanctuary, otherwise undistinguished.

WHERE TO EAT

Kendwa

Kendwa Rocks: Simple, reasonable-priced fish dishes, etc., good bar. Barbecues on beach when lots of people are around.

Sunset Bungalows: Limited but adequate menu, moderate prices, youthful atmosphere.

Titanic (Amaan Kendwa Beach Resort): Tables on the beach, simple but reasonable meals.

White Sands Beach Hotel: Stylish restaurant, menu brief but good with a vegetarian dish included.

Northern Unguja at a Glance

Nungwi

Various resorts have good to very good restaurants. Among the best of the cluster of specialist restaurants in west Nungwi are:

Cholo's: Rasta place on the beach, seemingly knocked together out of driftwood overnight, with an old motorbike, for reasons best known to Cholo, suspended from a nearby tree. Pilau, seafood, dinner on the beach by a campfire if you fancy it.

Fat Fish: Fine views from its wooden deck, high above the beach. Discos in the high season, when it can be quite lively. Offers a range of seafood and other dishes at similar, moderate prices.

New Blue Sea: Similar location to Fat Fish. Specializes in pizzas but serves seafood and other dishes. One of the better options in this vicinity.

Paradise: Again, in similar wonderful location, similarly priced menu with seafood and other dishes.

Z Hotel: In same cluster as restaurants above and said to be one of west Nungwi's best.

Matemwe

Matemwe Beach Village: Good restaurant.

Matemwe Bungalows: Long noted for its excellent seafood.

Mohammed Restaurant: Good, fresh, simple food.

Zanzibar Beach Resort: Large hotel with several restaurants.

Kiwengwa/Pwani Mchangani

This area has several super-resorts with their various good to excellent restaurants (none of them cheap), though lacking the intimacy and Zanzibari feel of some of the less formal places. If you prefer smaller, more casual places the restaurant at the Shooting Star Lodge has an enviable reputation.

Pongwe

Pongwe Beach Hotel: Almost the only option but this doesn't matter as the seafood is delicious.

Uroa

Jambo Beach Restaurant: Relaxed, simple. Good, reasonably priced food.

Tamarind Beach Hotel: Informal. Reasonable, simple.

Uroa White Villa: Good Swahili-style food.

Chwaka

Not much choice here. Chwaka Bay Resort has a huge restaurant if you can't wait until you reach Pongwe.

TOURS AND EXCURSIONS

A popular excursion in northern Unguja is the Spice Tour – among the best of which are those run by the Mitu family (off Malawi Rd, Malindi, tel: (0)24 223 4636). There are also, of course, many boat trips to various places for diving/snorkelling/fishing activities (see The Other Zanzibar chapter). Many hotels and resorts have dive and/or fishing centres where you can book such outings even if you're not staying there. There are cultural tours in certain villages, such as Nungwi (which would usually include the Turtle Aquarium there). Trips can also be arranged to Jozani Forest or Kizimkazi but from the extreme north these would be quite long and are best done from Stone Town or southern Unguja.

USEFUL CONTACTS

As for Stone Town, plus:
Dive/Water-sports Centres:
Kendwa/Nungwi
East Africa Diving and Water-sports Centre (Nungwi, tel: (0)777 416 425, (0)777 420 588;
Ras Nungwi Diving (Nungwi), tel: (0)24 223 3767;
Scuba Do (Kendwa), tel: (0)777 417 157;
Sensation Divers (Nungwi and Kendwa), tel: (0)745 863 634;
Zanzibar Water Sports (Nungwi and Kendwa), tel: (0)777 417 316.

Matemwe
One Ocean (Zanzibar Dive Centre), tel: (0)777 417 250;
Zanzibar Beach Resort, tel: (0)777 417 782.

Kiwengwa
One Ocean (Zanzibar Dive Centre), tel: (0)24 224 0241;
Pwani Mchangani, tel: (0)777 439 990.

5
Southern Unguja

Southern Unguja is generally far less fertile than its northern counterpart, though its western areas, and an extent of land just south of the central sector of Stone Town – Chwaka Road – have their share of luxuriant cultivation. South of Chwaka Bay, however, there is another important exception to the preponderance of coral rag, a remnant of moist indigenous forest at **Jozani**, best-known for its endemic Zanzibar red colobus monkeys.

As with the north, southern Unguja has few historical buildings of note outside Stone Town and its environs, but they include the ruins of **Dunga Palace** and the still functioning 12th-century mosque at **Kizimkazi Dimbani**, the site of one of Zanzibar's first continuously inhabited Shirazi settlements. Kizimkazi is also the centre for **dolphin-watching** activities and one of southern Unguja's many beach resorts, their white sands and almost fluorescent blue-green seas as prepossessing as any in the north.

Dunga Palace Ruins
Dunga Palace stands just south of the main Zanzibar Town-Chwaka road in central Unguja, 19km (12 miles) east of Stone Town. Unlike most of Zanzibar's palaces this one belonged to the last of the island's 'native' rulers, who, in fact, were descendents of Arab or Shirazi settlers and local women. The individuals of this ruling dynasty were known in Swahili as *Wawinyi Wakuu*.

DON'T MISS

★★★ At least two nights at a good **beach resort**.
★★ **Diving/snorkelling** at one of the sites along the reefs.
★★ **Jozani Forest**.
★ **Dolphin tour**.
★ Old mosque at **Kizimkazi**.
★ **Cultural tour** of one of the villages.
★ *Mwaka Kogwa* festival at Makunduchi if your visit coincides with it.

Opposite: *A Zanzibar red colobus monkey in the tree branches at Jozani Forest.*

DUNGA'S DARK SECRETS

Dunga Palace was built around a courtyard, Arab-style, and had two storeys, their windows fitted with coloured glass (now in the *Beit el-Ajaib*) and was surmounted by a rooftop garden. But this pleasant-sounding palace had its darker side. In the 1920s, as well as drums and horns (traditional 'badges of office' along the Swahili coast), more sinister souvenirs were unearthed; a nearby old well was half-choked with human skeletons. Dunga's master *Mwinyi Mkuu*, a descendant of the old 'Persian kings' of Shirazi Zanzibar, was apparently regarded (as was his palace) with a superstitious dread by his subjects.

MONKEY BUSINESS

Like all colobus the Zanzibar reds have stumps instead of thumbs ('colobus' means deformed, from the Greek *kolobos*) though this doesn't make them less acrobatic in the trees, where they feed mainly on young leaves (ignoring ripe fruit as they cannot digest sugars). One troop at Jozani-Chwaka feeds among exotic and cultivated trees outside the park boundary, and has surprisingly added charcoal, stolen from villagers' stockpiles, to its diet, perhaps to counteract toxic properties in certain leaves.

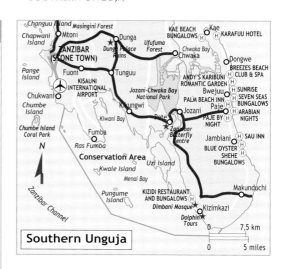

Southern Unguja

The palace is neither ancient nor spectacular (the ruins are mostly the product of a 1994 reconstruction programme) but they are pleasantly situated amid a grove of Indian almonds (*kungu*) and are interesting for the insight they give into the lifestyles of such local rulers. The *Mwinyi Mkuu* (Great Lord) who built the palace in the early 19th century was Hassan bin Ahmad al-Alawi and although his powers were diminished by the arrival of Sultan Said he was treated with respect and retained the right to dispense justice and demand taxes within his territory. He died in 1865, to be succeeded by his son Ahmad, who in turn was imprisoned (allegedly for tyranny) by Sultan Barghash in 1871, dying soon afterwards of smallpox. As there was no heir the dynasty came to an abrupt end.

JOZANI-CHWAKA BAY NATIONAL PARK

Many tourists stop off at **Jozani Forest** on their way to the southeastern beaches or the dolphin-watching centre at Kizimkazi, or as an excursion from Stone Town or elsewhere. Relatively few stop long enough to take full advantage of Jozani's possibilities, for most come mainly to see the forest's famous **Zanzibar red colobus monkeys** (*Procolobus kirkii*), isolated from related mainland red colobus for over a thousand years, thus evolving into a unique species, found only on Unguja. The highly social monkeys are attractively coloured, their rich reddish-brown napes and backs set off by a black band across the shoulders and whitish underparts, though their faces, dark with a splodge of pink under their noses and topped by a hair style that looks as if they have just grabbed a high voltage cable by accident, are never going to win first prize in a beauty contest. Uninformed locals believe the animals have toxic properties, which cause trees and crops to die when the primates have been feeding among them; they call the colobus *kima punju* (poison monkey).

The monkeys are not poisonous, of course, but they can become agitated if provoked at close quarters, when it is best to stay reasonably silent and avoid eye contact, moving back a little to reassure them. It is also advisable, however tempting, not to ask your driver to stop on the main road (alongside the park) so that you can observe and photograph the colobus that often feed there, as the driver will be fined if caught by the police. Apart from providing the lowly paid, often highly acquisitive police with *chai* money, this practice denies the park much-needed fees and robs visitors of a very rewarding experience inside the park, for there is much more to Jozani-Chwaka than the red colobus.

Other mammals include the near-endemic, much-endangered Ader's duiker (the size of a kid goat), the even smaller blue duiker and suni antelope, troops of blue monkeys, bushpigs, bushbabies, tree hyraxes, mongooses, squirrels and the Zanzibar giant rat. Bird life, as one might expect in a habitat that embraces moist tropical forest, coral rag forest and mangrove swamps, is varied and interesting, and includes endemic races of Fischer's Turaco, the Little Greenbul and the Mouse-coloured Sunbird, as well as two near-endemic races of the Eastern-bearded Scrub Robin and the Olive Sunbird.

Botanists or enthusiastic amateurs will delight in Jozani's mixture of indigenous and exotic trees and shrubs, among which are screw pine, Alexandrian laurel, palms, figs, eucalyptus, Indian almond, black plum and red

GIANT RAT WITH A GIANT HOUSE-MOVING PROBLEM

The Zanzibar giant rat (*Cricetomys gambianus cosensi*) can be as long as 1m (3ft) including the tail, but is more sinned against than sinning, apparently changing its burrow every two weeks to avoid being eaten. Exactly which predators in Jozani-Chwaka would take on a metre-long rat is a mystery, though maybe the rodent's 'collective unconscious' remembers the Zanzibar leopards that used to prowl around these parts but are probably now extinct.

SNAKES ALIVE!

The Zanzibar Land Animal Park (ZALA) is situated in the village of Mungoni, about 5km (3 miles) south of Jozani Forest on the Jozani-Kizimkazi road. A unique and successful example of sustainable development, it represents the realization of a dream by its originator and director, Mr Mohammed Ayoub Haji. Visitors to ZALA will find more than 25 species of snakes and lizards which are kept in enclosures rather than glass-fronted cages, allowing visitors (and the creatures themselves) to enjoy seeing (and being) animals in their natural habitat. The collection includes pythons, a Mozambique spitting cobra, boomslangs and a green mamba as well as smaller species.

Above: *Bottlenose dolphins at Kizimkazi.*

mahogany. One mahogany, thought to be over 200 years old, is known as *Mama Mtondoo* (Mother Mahogany). Your guide will also point out much else of interest, not least some of Jozani's diverse and colourful butterflies. These are at their abundant best during and just after the rains but passers-by should not ignore the **Zanzibar Butterfly Centre** at Pete, close to Jozani (just off the Zanzibar Town southern Unguja Road).

Nor should visitors to Jozani ignore the equally interesting salt marshes and mangrove swamps of the Chwaka Bay sector of the park. The nature trail that winds through the forest continues through this very different habitat via a boardwalk that begins about 1km (0.6 miles) south of the Jozani-Chwaka Bay National Park centre. The brackish water that flows among and around the roots of the mangroves is a nutritious nursery for fish and shellfish, as well as a natural home for crabs and other creatures, an environment that attracts a range of birds.

Swimming with the Dolphins

Many people who stop off at Jozani to see the red colobus also travel on to **Kizimkazi** to marvel at two other mammals, the **bottlenose** and **Indo-Pacific humpback dolphins** (the spinner dolphin also occurs in Zanzibar but is migratory). When arranging such a combined tour it is best to

---

FIXED SMILE AND OTHER FASCINATING FACTS

The dolphin's 'smile' is fixed; dolphins cannot move their facial muscles as we can. And they cannot breathe involuntarily, as we do – they have to decide to breathe. Which means that when they sleep, they have to keep one half of their brain awake. They cannot chew either; their many teeth are only used to grab prey. But they can hear much better than we can, and see perfectly well under or above the water. They also use echo-location, like bats, to hunt and navigate.

travel to Kizimkazi first and stop off at Jozani later in the day, staying at Kizimkazi overnight. This allows you to hire a boat and go looking for the dolphins before everyone else turns up. Otherwise you might find yourself among a flotilla of boats that bear down upon any unfortunate dolphin like the Spanish Armada high on sherry. Not a pretty sight as half the boats' passengers, not all built like Greek gods or goddesses, leap overboard to swim with the dolphins when the opportunity presents itself. The dolphins, understandably alarmed, make off with rather more grace and less noise.

You could try asking your boat's skipper not to chase the dolphins, or you might try hiring a boat to take you on a longer trip into nearby **Menai Bay**, now a conservation area created in 1997, as a 'gift to the earth'. There is a good chance of seeing dolphins very close to Kizimkazi, especially on calm days; the chances out in Menai Bay are about one in five as there is a greater area to cover, though the boat crews know where to look. In any case, the bay is attractive enough, with its flanking peninsulas and various islets (volcanic in origin), and you will avoid the crowds.

Boat trips into Menai Bay may also be organized from **Ras Fumba**, a small village at the southern tip of the Fumba Peninsula, only 18km (11 miles) from Stone Town. Surprisingly this fertile peninsula is hardly visited by tourists, though its pleasant little beach (not quite so white as those at Nungwi and on the east coast) now has its first, and equally pleasant, tourist lodge.

Back in Kizimkazi, there are other distractions, and in fact two villages in one: Dimbani, where

Below: *An old Shirazi mosque building in Kizimkazi.*

Above: *Breezes Beach Club is a large, walled luxury resort.*

NINE CENTURIES OF PRAYERS...

Dimbani Mosque looks quite ordinary from outside, with its corrugated-iron roof, but the interior, despite extensive rebuilding in 1770, retains much of its original Persian atmosphere and form, particularly the wall incorporating the mihrab, all of which is original. Visitors might sometimes share the mosque with one or two men at prayer, for the lovely old place is still in use. It is a humbling experience for many non-Muslims, and a far cry from the negative view of 'fundamental Islam' that many Westerners espouse.

most dolphin tours start and end, and Mkunguni. The settlement (originally established by Persian merchants from Shirazi) goes back to the 12th century at least, as its best-known building, the **Dimbani Mosque**, bears witness. An inscription in flowery Kufic alongside the original mihrab (the niche from where the Imam leads the prayers) proclaims that the mosque was commissioned 'by Sheikh Abuu Amran bin Mussa Ibn Mohammed, May God grant him long life and destroy his enemy' and is dated AH500 (AD1107). What happened to Abuu Amran or his enemy is unspecified but the graves outside the mosque contain the remains of another sheikh who was 'pious' and 'single-handed', a 'one-legged Sayyid Abdalla', Mwana the daughter of Mmadi and her son Mfaume Ali Omar, keeper of the town drum (now on display in the *Beit el-Ajaib* in Stone Town).

Other traces of the original Shirazi settlement, probably the remnants of the walls of a fort, can be seen not far away, and Kizimkazi was also, at one time, the seat of a *Mwinyi Mkuu* (one of Zanzibar's traditional rulers), whilst at Kizimkazi Mkunguni stand **two baobabs**, the larger of which is thought to be 600 years old. More modern buildings and trees, a few small resorts and restaurants among the palms and casuarinas, stand nearby, for Kizimkazi is popular not only with dolphin enthusiasts but because of its glaringly white (if not too private) beaches.

THE BEACHES OF SOUTHERN UNGUJA

As with the north, it is the beaches of southern Unguja that attract most visitors, and with good reason. In the west they are restricted to the one already mentioned at Ras Fumba and a few others (as yet undeveloped) around Menai Bay and the eastern edge of Pete Inlet, as well as those at Kizimkazi. But in the east the inevitably white sands and outlying coral shelf stretch in an almost unbroken line from the Michamvi Peninsula in the north to the southern extremes of Jambiani, 25km (15.5 miles) down the Sunrise Coast.

Michamvi

The narrow arm of **Michamvi Peninsula** acts as a natural sea-break along the eastern confines of **Chwaka Bay**. Not that the squarish bay is a good harbour, except for the fishing boats that work out of it, as it is clogged with mangroves along most of its shores. The waters of the bay overlie a broad bed of coral, though the locality is not particularly appealing, with one notable exception on the northwestern headland of the Michamvi Peninsula.

It is here that the tiny fishing village of **Kae** stands, 1km (0.6 miles) north of Michamvi Village. One day this peaceful little corner will no doubt become another tasteless monument to some developer's ego, but for now you can almost hear the ghost crabs whisper across the powdery white sands, and see the subtle shifts in the blues and greens and turquoises of the sea as the light changes. Not that the beach at Kae is perfect; it has its share of seaweed (in fact seaweed is farmed here, as elsewhere along the southeastern coast) and of natural jetsam. And there are as yet no moon-raves or disco music or infinity pools and jacuzzis to wallow in while your overpriced cocktail is being shaken. But if you crave tranquility and natural beauty, and a simple place in which to sleep and eat, Kae is as good as any. If you get tired of lying around on the sand in the shade of a palm you can take a boat tour around the mangrove swamps, a little further south, and work up an appetite for dinner.

> ## WHITER THAN WHITE
>
> The colour and texture of sand beaches around the world depends on the nature of local rocks or other materials that, when eroded, make up the sand, but even within Zanzibar there are variations, depending, once again, on local conditions. White 'coral' beaches are in fact created by the bio-erosion of limestone skeletal material of various types, such as molluscs or crustaceans, of which corals are not usually even predominant. Much of the coral that is found in the sand of tropical beaches has an interesting, if not altogether attractive, history, having passed through the gut of millions of parrotfish over the millennia. The parrotfish, which feed on living corals, excrete the inorganic skeletal matter, which being limestone is basically white.

Female seaweed farmers from several villages in Unguja now operate as a group under the Zanzibar Seaweed Cluster Initiative, set up in 2006 with the support of various local and international agencies. Seaweeds farmed, as in Zanzibar generally, are mainly *Eucheuma denticulatum* and *Kappaphycus alvarezii* and to a smaller extent *K. striatum*, but the Cluster has initiated a new method of farming, using deeper water-floating lines to combat die-offs among the *Kappaphycus* plants. Seaweeds are made into all kinds of products (*see* panel, page 80) and the Zanzibar Cluster, which already makes soap, might soon be producing shampoo and even biscuits. The Kidoti chapter of the Cluster (based a few kilometres south of Nungwi in northern Unguja) also produces spice soaps of cinnamon, clove, eucalyptus, sweet basil, and lemon grass. In fact, the Seaweed Cluster has a remarkable history as a spin-off from research and development and is also helping to raise the personal quality of life and aspirations among poor women and their children.

Just around the corner of the headland the more developed but no less exquisite southeastern beaches unwind in a narrowing and seemingly endless white band, and to save repetition, the white is genuinely white and the colours in the sea are, in the right light, almost surreal. Of course there is variation – the beach and its outlying coral shelf are narrower in some areas, broader in others, here the beach is backed by palms, there by casuarinas – but basically it's holiday brochure stuff all the way down to the southern extremes of Jambiani. As with the northern sector of the Sunrise Coast the coral shelf (almost 3km/2 miles broad at Jambiani) is left exposed at low tide, limiting swimming in most places to about two six-hour periods every 24 hours, but providing interesting rock pool rambles and allowing you to see and photograph (please ask permission) the local seaweed farmers and harvesters.

The raised east coast of Michamvi descends to the sea in a tumble of fossil coral, on the bulldozer-subdued slopes and terraces of which stand several large resorts, the everything-under-one-roof package tour places that some people enjoy and others find abhorrent. Within their enclosing walls you and hundreds of others can enjoy your holiday without being bothered by *papasi* or worrying about being abducted, robbed or otherwise molested, and imagine you are in Italy. To be fair, these places sometimes have a spurious grandeur, however ostentatious and impersonal; perhaps they are no worse, in their way, than some of Barghash's palaces.

Opposite the mid-sector of the peninsula's eastern seaboard is a channel through the coral shelf, officially called the Pass of Dongwe, more commonly **the Lagoon**. At low tide, with the channel still flowing north to south between broad banks of sand, you could almost imagine (if you were looking out from a fridge) that you are in Antarctica rather than Unguja, the sand is so white. The lagoon provides good fishing and snorkelling, as well as a passage through the reef. Around and between the large, expensive or relatively expensive resorts two or three simple but pleasant, value-for-money restaurants have somehow found a niche.

Michamvi phases imperceptibly into **Bwejuu** about 5km (3 miles) north of the small fishing community of Bwejuu Village. This sector of the beach is as beautiful as any, though its 15 or so hotels, guesthouses and resorts are generally much more low-key and intimate than those further north, in some cases simple to the point of eccentricity. There are resorts without walls or even, in most cases, fences, where you and Zanzibar come together like the sea and the sand, and feel that you belong. Most don't have swimming pools and don't always provide direct access to diving, snorkelling, fishing or other water sports, but you can swim in the sea, when the tide is in, and book other activities through the nearest hotel that offers them. Bicycles can be hired from almost anywhere, allowing you to ride along the beach as the locals do.

Four kilometres (2.5 miles) south of Bwejuu Village is the larger, more picturesque village of **Paje**. The whitish coral rock that is used for house-building along

Below: *Seaweed is farmed on the coast south of Paje.*

Above: *The process of drying seaweed in the sun takes a few days.*

SENSATIONAL SEAWEEDS

Seaweeds are sensational; they are used in the production of certain ice creams, toothpastes, de-icing fluids, cheeses, paints, pancake syrups, breads, paper finishes, salad dressings, beers, pastas, tomato sauces, fruit juices, skin creams, canned meats, printed textiles, baby foods, swimming pool filters, lipsticks, air fresheners, peanut butters, whipped toppings, antacids, fire and sound insulations, creamers, explosives and, last but not least, adhesives to keep your false teeth from falling out.

Zanzibar's east coast is not intrinsically attractive, especially when the houses are ranged monotonously along the main track in a kind of rural ribbon development, as many are. The houses in Paje are not particularly prepossessing either, in isolation, yet the village has a disorderly, amicable, shoulder-to-shoulder charm and particular corners are quite photogenic. Its seafront certainly is, with sands the colour and consistency of powdered milk, backed by palms in places and stretching all the way to the reef. Which means that when the light and tide is right, the sea at Paje is a rapturous band of turquoise.

Six kilometres (4 miles) or so to the south of Paje is **Jambiani**, which seems to go on and on. Situated amid a grove of palms, it is not as compact or picturesque as Paje, though it is a friendly enough place and its extensive beach bears comparison with most. The coral flats off Jambiani are particularly broad, making a trek to the reef at low tide quite daunting in the heat of the day, especially as you have to sidestep the rock pools with their spiky clusters of sea urchins (common throughout Zanzibar wherever rock pools occur).

There are compensations. Jambiani, like other suitable places along Unguja's east coast, is a centre for seaweed farming, and it is worth walking out across the coral shelf at low tide to take a look at this unusual form of cultivation. As the tide recedes lines of short stakes, arranged in parallel rows, are exposed, linked by cords on which clumps of seaweed (*mwani*) hang like washing on a line. Farming and harvesting the seaweed is traditionally but not exclusively the work of women. Two types of seaweed are grown in this intertidal zone, planted by attaching seedlings to the cords and harvested about six weeks later (three weeks when a strong northeaster is blowing). If you are sensitive the women will let you watch them work and (perhaps for a small fee) take photographs. The harvested seaweed is stuffed into sacks and taken ashore to be sun-dried for several days. In places like Jambiani you will come across subtly coloured spreads of it, in faded green, purple, old gold and russet, like giant lichens beautifying the ground.

Seaweed farming is a gruelling business in the searing heat and dehydrating winds out on the sands and coral flats, as half an hour or so in the vicinity will convince you. But it will give you an insight into just how poor and tough many Zanzibaris are, and yet how generally cheerful and welcoming in spite of everything. More insights into village life can be gained by taking a cultural tour, which includes seaweed farming as well as visits to local herbalists, schools and other scenes of day-to-day events in such communities.

Should you take an excursion from Jambiani to Kizimkazi to see the dolphins you will pass through **Makunduchi**, an unprepossessing town, though it has, just to the east, a pleasant enough beach and a large, Italian-orientated resort. Passing through is what most tourists do, though in the third or fourth week of July the town changes character as it celebrates the New Year. Not because everything comes late in Zanzibar (which is often the case), nor does everyone stand around looking sheepish and singing *Auld Lang Syne*, for this particular new year festival (**Mwaka Kogwa**) was introduced by Zoroastrian immigrants from Persia over a thousand years ago. It lasts for four days (*see* panel, this page).

HAPPY NEW YEAR

Mwaka Kogwa (Washing the Year) celebrates the end of the harvest as well as the beginning of a new year. Its climax comes when a *mganga* (medicine man) builds a thatched hut, accompanied by singing women. A group of village elders enters the hut, which is set alight by the *mganga*. The elders play to the gallery by delaying their exit to the last minute, when they hopefully emerge unscathed. Mock fights between two groups of men, using sticks or banana stalks, follow, causing further ribaldry, before the festival settles into four days of feasting (and covert drinking).

Southern Unguja at a Glance

Mid-May to mid-October, when temperatures and humidity lowest and rainfall usually minimal, though all other times of year outside the long rains (approx. mid-March to mid-May) can be enjoyable. Mid-October to mid-March can sometimes be uncomfortably hot and humid, sometimes with showers, but off-sea breezes help to counteract this and diving is at its best during this period.

Taxis are frequently used (haggle beforehand) but a cheaper alternative is to take a **'tourist' mini-bus** from outside the Old Fort in Stone Town or wherever else (ask at your hotel but shop around if you have the time and patience). Such mini-buses are usually clean, comfortable and efficient though you will usually have to share them (hence the lower costs) with other tourists and they might not always leave on time (they tend to have at least two departure times but do not operate after about 13:00 or 14:00). Zanzibaris usually get around by *dala-dala* (see Around Stone Town at a Glance). They tend to be crowded.

Most people tend to stay within walking distance of their resorts or hire bicycles,

though taxis are often available. Boats are of course provided by resorts, water-sports centres, etc. for scuba-diving/snorkelling enthusiasts or for trips to outlying islets.

Kae
BUDGET
Kae Beach Bungalows, tel: (0)777 475 299/487 723, www.kaebeachbungalows. com Best of Kae's present options. Basic but comfortable and superbly peaceful and beautiful location. As in all Zanzibar's smaller hotels and guesthouses, order meals (and sometimes even cold beers) well in advance.

Dongwe
LUXURY
Breezes Beach Club & Spa, reservations (Nairobi) tel: +254 20 272 0835/9333/ 8826, email: info@breezes-zanzibar.com www.breezes-zanzibar.com One of the larger, less personal, walled resorts but with all mod-cons. **Karafuu Hotel**, tel: (0)777 413 647/8, email: info@ karafuuhotel.com www. karafuuhotel.com Large, walled hotel, but welcoming and stylish.

Bwejuu
MID-RANGE
Andy's Karibuni Romantic Garden, tel: (0)748 430 942, www.eastzanzibar.com Unsophisticated but warm and

welcoming with excellent food and the fine beach that is common to all these Bwejuu resorts. Little below mid-range. **Palm Beach Inn**, tel: (0)24 224 0221, (0)777 411 155, email: mahfudh28@ hotmail.com Cluster of simple rooms by the beach, south of Bwejuu Village. Welcoming and well run but restaurant has a reputation for being over-priced. **Sunrise Hotel**, tel: (0)777 415 240/486 350, email: sunrise@zanlink.com www. sunrise-zanzibar.com An intimate and (in a very individualistic way) charming little place run by an equally individualistic and charming Belgian expatriate. Unlike many hotels in the area the Sunrise has a swimming pool, and superb French-style food. Little way north of the village.

BUDGET
Robinson's Place, tel: (0)777 413 479, (0)748 595 572, www.robinsonsplace.net Bit eccentric but if you like unusual, laid-back and warm places that don't cost an arm and a leg this is worth considering. One of its rooms, by the beach, looks as if Robinson (Crusoe that is) has just left. Little way north of the village. **Seven Seas Bungalows**, tel: (0)777 481 767. Cheap and cheerful what-you-see-is-what-you-get kind of place south of the village.

Southern Unguja at a Glance

Paje
MID-RANGE TO BUDGET
Arabian Nights Hotel, tel:
(0)24 224 0190/1, email:
anights@pajedivecentre.com
www.zanzibararabiannights.
com Compact little hotel with
rooms, each with their own
private balconies, in four adjacent bungalows (best rooms
have sea view) but welcoming
and good value. On seaward
edge of Paje Village, overlooking delightful seascape.
Dive centre.
Paje By Night, tel:
(0)777 460 710, www.
pajebynight.net Set back
from the beach but a friendly,
hospitable place with an easy-
going, individualistic charm.
Excellent bar and restaurant.
Paradise Beach Bungalows,
tel: (0)24 223 1387, tel:
(0)777 414 129, www.
geocities.jp/paradisebeach
bungalows Friendly, quiet
little resort among a grove of
coconuts, very good value if
you don't expect luxuries
(like electricity) but value
good food. Courses in Swahili
cooking, as well as dhow
trips and cultural tours.

Jambiani
MID-RANGE TO BUDGET
Sau Inn, tel: (0)24 224 0205,
(0)777 457 782, www.
sauinn.net Medium-sized,
attractive colonial-style hotel
with a swimming pool (not
common in this area) and
pleasant little gardens. Needs
some managerial inspiration

but very friendly staff, good,
simple food and (overall)
good value for money.
Blue Oyster, tel: (0)24 224
0163, email: blueoysterhotel
@gmx.de www.zanzibar.de
Small family-run (German)
hotel with thatched roof and
restaurant and bar on the
broad first-storey balcony
overlooking sea. Set among
palms by fine beach. Good
value for money.
**Mount Zion Long Beach
Bungalows**, tel: (0)777 439
034/439 001, www.
mountzion-zanzibar.com
Relaxed (Rasta-style) little
place on grassy headland
between Jambiani and Paje,
with partial views of the sea
(bordered by wonderful
beach). *Bandas* (thatched
huts) imaginatively designed.

BUDGET
Shehe Bungalows, tel: (0)24
223 3949, tel: (0)777 418
386, email:shehebungalows@
hotmail.com Just south of
Jambiani Village. Clean, comfortable cottages facing the
sea, either side of main building, which has lovely views
from its first-floor restaurant
and bar. Good value for
money.

Kizimkazi (Dimbani)
LOWER MID-RANGE
**Kizidi Restaurant and
Bungalows**, tel: (0)777 417
053. On northern headland
alongside the bay, this is the
best of Kizimkazi's hotels.

Wonderful views from all five
rooms. Restaurant popular
with day trippers but pricey.

WHERE TO EAT

Kizimkazi
Cabs Restaurant (Kizimkazi
Dimbani). Cheaper alterna-
tive to Kidizi.
Kidizi Restaurant (Kizimkazi
Dimbani). Reasonable but
expensive for what you get.
Pomboo's Restaurant
(Kizimkazi Mkunguni).
Pleasant seafront location and
(appropriately) good seafood
for the price.

TOURS AND EXCURSIONS

The obvious one is the
dolphin tour (you could also
go to **Jozani Forest**). As with
northern Unguja there are
centres at certain resorts that
organize **boat trips for
diving/snorkeling/fishing
activities** (see chapter entitled
The Other Zanzibar).

USEFUL CONTACTS

As for Stone Town, plus:
Zanzibar Butterfly Centre,
www.zanzibarbutterflies.com
Paje Dive Centre (Arabian
Nights Hotel, Paje), tel:
(0)24 224 0190/91, tel:
(0)777 416 614, email:
paje@pajedivecentre.com
Rising Sun Dive Centre
(Breezes Beach Club & Spa,
Dongwe), tel: (0)777 415
049; **Scuba Do Dive Centre**
(Fumba Beach Lodge, Fumba
Peninsula), www.scuba-do-
zanzibar.com

6
Pemba,
Isle of Mystery

Pemba has been called the Green Island and the Isle of Cloves, but it might well be called the **Isle of Mystery**, as it is little visited by outsiders and almost completely undeveloped for tourism. Once relatively rich, Pemba has since languished, neglected by the authorities on Unguja (including the sultans and the British) and on the Tanzanian mainland. Despite or because of all this the island is quite fascinating to those visitors who don't mind travelling in a crowded *dala-dala* and who are prepared to forego a few luxuries with regard to accommodation.

Not that Pemba doesn't have its luxuries, though there aren't many and a few nights in the most exclusive of them (intended mainly for divers and snorkellers) will set your bank balance back quite a bit. The island's diving and fishing, however, are said to be among the best in the world, and together with snorkelling represent Pemba's major tourist attractions.

Pemba will not remain mysterious for long. Its capital, **Chake Chake**, is no Stone Town and its two other main towns, Mkoani and Wete, are hardly New York or Paris, but they are all interesting in their own low-key, Islamic way, as are Pemba's scattered historic ruins. And Pemba's beaches, though far fewer and generally smaller and less accessible than those on Unguja, are often exquisite, and exquisitely secluded. Pemba even has its own equivalent of Mnemba Island, Misali, with its own delightful little beaches (open to everyone, unlike those on Mnemba), and its own glorious snorkelling and diving opportunities. It also has its equivalent of Jozani Forest, **Ngezi**, though

DON'T MISS

★★★ **Diving/fishing/ snorkelling** from one of the dive/fishing lodges.
★★★ **Boat trip** to Misali Island (for diving/snorkelling/ picnic/nature ramble) via Quanbalu Ruins.
★★ Guided walk through **Ngezi Forest** (three stars for this if you are a keen birder/naturalist).
★ **Cultural tour** of town/ village.
★ Stroll around **Chake Chake**.
★ **Pujini Ruins**.
★ **Bullfight**.

Opposite: *A typically dramatic African sunset.*

WHERE THE CLOVE WAS KING

Pemba was always the true Isle of Cloves but there are calls now to liberalize the market as disillusioned farmers lose interest in tending the plantations due (among other things) to declining prices. Production has fallen steadily over recent years (between 2003 and 2007 from 5896 to 3998 tonnes) and smuggling of cloves, sometimes, allegedly, by certain high-ranking officials, has increased. The crop, which once provided 65% of the government's earnings, now accounts for below 10%. Despite this, cloves are still very much in evidence in Pemba. The cloves are harvested between July and December, when pickers climb the trees, which can attain heights of 15m (49ft), using ropes or ladders, snapping off clusters of unopened buds, greenish or yellowish red. These are collected in baskets and laid out in the sun for four to seven days until their colour deepens to the familiar dark brown, when they are graded and packed for export. Or, it seems, smuggled. There is, incidentally, an essential oils factory a short drive east of Chake Chake where inter-ested visitors can see clove oil being produced.

Right: *Local women browsing and buying goods at Chake Chake market.*

more remote, with a number of endemic or near-endemic animals, birds and plants.

If you like mysteries, challenges and adventure (on, by or under the sea) and can manage without eggs Benedict for breakfast or oysters and champagne on your picnics, you will like Pemba, but if you can't live without life's luxuries and can afford them, try the up-market lodges.

UNPRETENTIOUS URBANITY: PEMBA'S MAIN TOWNS

Unless you fly to Pemba you will almost certainly arrive, via the ferry from Dar es Salaam or Stone Town, at **Mkoani**, the island's biggest port (don't expect Sydney Harbour) in the southwest. The area around the waterfront just to the south of the jetty, with its fish and other markets, is the town's most interesting feature, and for most of us the only one. For visitors with time to spare and who don't mind walking there is an attractive sand spit about 4km (2.5 miles) north of the town at **Ras Mkoasha**, a hike that will bring you into passing contact with some of Mkoani's inhabitants and hopefully confirm their genuinely welcoming nature.

Chake Chake

Pemba's capital, **Chake Chake**, lies beyond the rumpled green country some 28 or so kilometres (17 miles) to the northeast. The journey, which is normally by local mini-bus (*dala-dala*) or clapped-out taxi, takes you between rice

paddies and on through extensive clove plantations, one of the most attractive routes in Pemba.

Despite being Pemba's largest town you can walk around the centre of Chake Chake without breaking sweat, and although it is far less historic and interesting than Stone Town, its old Omani quarter has the same deceptively timeless atmosphere and a dilapidated but authentic Eastern appeal, made even more authentic by the odd bullock cart.

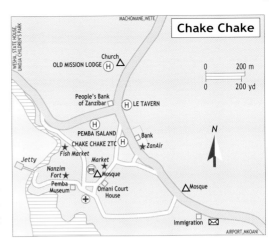

Chake Chake

Nanzim Fort

Apart from this sometimes photogenic little area, Chake Chake's most interesting landmark is the much-diminished **Nanzim Fort**, built on the modest heights above the town commanding a view of the mangrove-lined creek to the west, with its sometimes splendid sunsets. The fort was established by the Portuguese before being restructured, in the 18th century, by the Omanis, who kept faith with the fort's original square towers despite their traditional preference for round ones. Much of the fort was demolished early in the 20th century to make way for the hospital, the fort's remnants serving as a prison and then a police barracks before falling into disuse. A section of what remains is now an interesting little museum, displaying artefacts and information about various aspects of life in Pemba.

Also worthy of closer scrutiny, if you are a keen birder, are the little niches in the fort's outer walls, for the pretty little **Java sparrow** (an introduced species now declining in its native land) has adapted to life there. With its disproportionately large, sealing-wax red bill, its black head and white cheek patches, the finch is easily recognizable and usually easily observed and photographed.

PEMBA REVEALED

A sector of what remains of Nanzim Fort is now a small but attractive museum (open, for a small fee, on Mon–Fri from 08:30–16:30, and on Sat and Sun from 09:00–16:00). It boasts only three small rooms but they contain informative and interesting displays showing various aspects of Pemba and its history, with explanatory notes in English and Swahili. One room is devoted to Pemba's various ruins and archeological sites, together with a display of artefacts, including coins and medieval pottery. A second room is concerned with dhows and seafaring matters, including fishing, and a third is given over to Zanzibar's rulers, and their influence, for better or for worse, on Pemba.

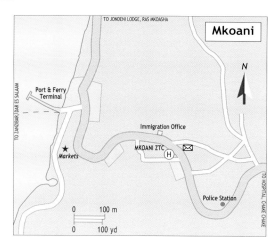

Sights in Chake Chake

Other places of interest in Chake Chake include the **market**, in the town centre, where you can buy herbs, spices, clove honey and one of Zanzibar's traditional sweetmeats, *halua*; a nearby **old mosque** with a rounded minaret; and the architecturally pleasing, pre-Independence **Omani Court House** with a fine carved door and clock tower (the clock, appropriately in timeless Chake Chake, having long abandoned any ambitions with regard to the exposition of passing hours). There is a **State House** also, secreted away among its gardens and, like many such places, jealously guarded and off limits to all but the high and mighty and their guests. Nearby is the **Umoja Children's Park** which only opens at Eid ul-Fitr and other holidays, even Christmas Day.

One of Chake Chake's main advantages is its central location in what is after all a rather small island. It is fairly easy, if not always comfortable, to travel between here and Pemba's two other main towns, **Mkoani** in the southwest and **Wete** in the northwest, or even to go beyond Wete to the extreme northwest, where there are two good lodges, some beautiful beaches and the interesting **Ngezi Forest** (though all this is best achieved, if you are not staying at one of the lodges, by basing yourself in Wete).

Pujini Ruins

Ten kilometres (6 miles) southeast of Chake Chake, near Pujini Village, are the **Pujini Ruins**, the remains of a 15th-century fortified enclosure and ramparts, which together covered about 15ha (37 acres), linked to the nearby east coast by a small canal. It is said to be the only known early fortification along the East African seaboard. The ruins are now little more than rubble but standing as they do, among a

---

INDIAN GHOST TOWN

Among Pemba's scattered ruins is a relatively recent but still interesting site at Jambangome, just northeast of Mkoani. In the 19th century this was one of the main settlements on Pemba, occupied by Indian immigrants, those unsung pioneers whose contribution to East Africa's economy and development is often overlooked. The best-preserved building along Jambangome's old main street is a Bohra mosque.

grove of baobabs and tamarinds, are quite picturesque. This, together with the history of the place and one or two surviving features, makes the trip worthwhile, though the ruins are not easy to find and perhaps the best option is a specific half-day trip from Chake Chake in a hired car. You could go by bicycle but would need to find a knowledgeable guide in Pujini to lead you to the ruins and explain their significance.

The fortifications were once the headquarters of a so-called Persian prince (which some interpret as tyrant, merchant and pirate), Mohammad bin Abdulrahman, the descendent, like most of his **Wadiba** subjects, of Shirazi settlers. He not only ruled the area but perhaps the whole of Pemba with legendary cruelty. He was apparently, however, a committed Muslim (as well as a capable boat-builder and expert bowman) and the well-preserved **mosque**, outside the fortified enclosure, was built later by bin Abdulrahman as a gesture of goodwill or reconciliation towards the citizens he was said to have terrified. Descendants of the Imam that he appointed are still connected with the mosque, and worshippers come from as far afield as Unguja.

Other structures still visible include the fortress ramparts and a staircase leading to them, a subterranean chamber, a shrine and traces of the old channel north of the enclosure. There is also a well, said to have been divided by a wall to keep two of the tyrant's wives (who were intensely jealous of each other) out of face-scratching range. Women intent on shredding each other's faces, however, would surely have legged it around the well (and the wall) in order to do so, and the wall probably had a more innocent purpose.

Vitongoji

A little way northeast of Pujini and about 8km (5 miles) east of Chake Chake is the village of **Vitongoji**, 2 or 3km (1 or 2 miles) beyond which is a series of small white-sand coves, where you can swim if the tide is in or go rock-pool rambling if it is out. You can probably hire a *dala-dala* in Chake Chake or take the regular *dala-dala* to Vitongoji and walk the extra 2.5km (1.5 miles) to the shore. A better alternative if you're feeling up to it is to hire a bicycle; just remember that cycling in Pemba's climate can be dehydrating.

GRASPER OF MEN

Mohammad bin Abdulrahman, master of Pujini, was known as *Mkama Ndume* (Grasper of Men), which leaves little to the imagination; his cruelty was legendary, as stories passed down through the generations seem to testify. It is said that 40 years after his death grown men, still fearful of his reputation, could be made to work against their will merely by the invocation of his name.

Quanbalu Ruins

A much more memorable trip from Chake Chake is to hire a boat to take you to one of Pemba's most attractive loca-tions, Misali Island, 17km (10.5 miles) due west, prefer-ably taking in the ruined settlement of **Quanbalu** on the way. The ruins lie close to the village of Ngagu on the terminal blob of the **Ras Mkumbuu Peninsula**, that reaches out along the northern edge of Chake Chake Creek. It is possible to get there by road, though most drivers are not too enthusiastic (try Jambo Tours & Safaris at Le-Tavern Hotel in town).

Quanbalu, the oldest known Islamic settlement in East Africa, might have been established as early as the 8th century, though this is debated. It was certainly flourishing during the 11th century, when it was thought to have been one of the largest Swahili settlements along the East African coast. The Arabian adventurer al-Masudi visited the town in AD916 and revealed that among its Muslim citizens were 'Zanj infidels' with scant regard for orthodox religious beliefs, worshipping whatever took their fancy, 'be it a plant, an animal, or a mineral'. The Muslims were apparently descended from religious refugees, who became locally powerful and presumably prosperous, for pottery from Arabia and Persia and a soapstone bowl from Madagascar are among the artefacts uncovered there, as well as a Chinese coin.

The ruins, though built on older foundations, are mostly from the 13th and 14th centuries, and are perhaps the best-preserved ruins in the Zanzibar archipelago. They include the remains of the largest ancient mosque in Pemba (once the largest in sub-Saharan Africa), with a minaret and a mihrab, simply but pleasingly carved, plus the remains of houses and several graves. Some graves are in the form of pillar tombs, typical of the period and characteristically decorated with Chinese porcelain bowls, these embellish-ments presumably indicative of the importance of the tombs' occupants. The town fell into decline in the 16th century and was enigmatically abandoned. This mystery, and the setting of the ruins on this rather lonely peninsula, lend a wistful but not unpleasant atmosphere to the site.

MISALI ISLAND

Less wistful and even more interesting is the delectable little island of **Misali**, only 6km (4 miles) from the nearest point of Ras Mkumbuu. Misali rose from the depths an estimated 15,000 years ago, a treasure island in more ways than one, for the notorious pirate Captain Kidd is rumoured to have buried his ill-gotten loot here. Another legend reveals that a prophet called Hadara, needing a prayer mat but finding none, used the little island instead. You might not find Captain Kidd's treasure but if you dive or snorkel you will discover a whole jewellery box of gems beneath Misali's clear blue seas, which is why the island was declared a marine sanctuary in 1996.

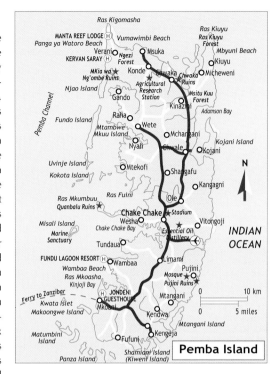

Misali also has several nature trails, none of them too demanding (the island itself is only 2km/1 mile long). One trail is intertidal, another through the mangroves, one between two beaches and a fourth takes you to one of Misali's three sacred caves, each inhabited by more or less friendly spirits, though they might get a bit upset if you walk in half-naked. Each cave has its traditional healer who keeps the spirits company and presumably does whatever is necessary with the various offerings that are brought to the caves by Pemba's superstitious citizens.

Among Misali's natural assets are many corals and species of fish, **green** and **hawksbill turtles** (which nest here), huge nocturnal **coconut crabs**, a rare subspecies of monkey (the **Pemba vervet monkey**) and colonies of

Here's Lookin' at Ya, Kidd

Captain William Kidd was born in Scotland around 1645 but moved to New York, where he became a successful merchant and privateer. Whilst commanding a ship in the Indian Ocean, with a mission to fight piracy, he turned pirate himself. Eventually he returned to New York hoping for a king's pardon but was arrested and sent for trial to London. After a year in the notorious Newgate Prison he was hanged (the rope broke the first time) at Execution Dock. His body was tarred and hung in chains for several years.

endangered fruit bats (**Pemba flying foxes**). You need to be keen to give yourself a good chance of seeing the monkeys, as they are extremely shy, feeding on ghost crabs (often on the western beaches) in the quiet of the early morning, before most tourists arrive. Which means leaving Chake Chake before sunrise; earlee earlee catchee monkey.

A small fee, called the *pecca* fee, is charged for visiting Misali, as it is for all marine activities along the west coast. It helps to pay for the island's conservation and for the **visitors' centre** on Baobab Beach, where the tour boats land. The centre has informative displays on the island's ecology and useful wildlife and information sheets. There are no resorts or accommodation of any kind on the islet, nor facilities for camping, and alcohol is prohibited.

Wete

From Chake Chake a good road now heads towards northern Pemba, passing through cultivated land, flatter than the country further south though just as luxuriant, with intermittent but extensive patches of forest and large rice paddies, bringing you into **Wete** after about an hour. Your first glimpse of the town, if you come by road, involves housing blocks that look as if they were ordered by 'Uncle Joe' Stalin on one of his less avuncular days. As with many unprepossessing towns, however, Wete's friendly people make up for its more-than-parochial nature and on closer acquaintance it has a modest charm. Its port lies at the foot of a steep hill and as with many waterfronts is the town's focal point. There is little to enthuse the casual visitor, except for two fish markets, said to have been established to keep rival groups of fishermen at arm's length.

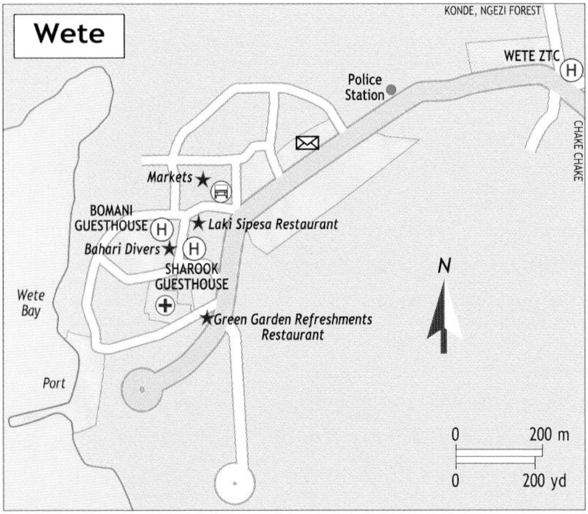

Wete
KONDE, NGEZI FOREST
WETE ZTC
Police Station
CHAKE CHAKE
Markets
BOMANI GUESTHOUSE
Laki Sipesa Restaurant
Bahari Divers
SHAROOK GUESTHOUSE
N
Wete Bay
Green Garden Refreshments Restaurant
Port
0
200 m
0
200 yd

PEMBA'S INDIGENOUS FORESTS

Few non-Pembans wind up in Wete but many of those who do come to visit a most fascinating area of original moist forest (Ngezi), some heavenly beaches and a first-class tourist lodge, **Manta Reef**, as well as a friendly, more modest resort, **Kervan Saray**.

Ngezi Forest

Ngezi Forest covers 1440ha (3558 acres) and is one of the last remnants of the natural forests that covered much of Pemba until the mid-19th century, when they were hacked down to make way for clove plantations. It was established as a protected forest reserve in the 1950s, with good reason, for many of its plants and animals are endemic, near-endemic or extremely interesting, even to non-specialists.

Despite being located at the coast, the mainland equivalents of some of its trees, such as *Quassia undulata*, only occur in lowland mountain forests. Other trees found in Ngezi (e.g. *Musa acuminata* and *Typhanodorun lindleyanum*) have counterparts in Southeast Asia or Madagascar. The forest also contains exotics, some of which (e.g. *Muesopsis eminii*) have become intrusive. The origin of other species is another Pemban mystery.

Approximately half of the reserve comprises lush moist forest with a dense under-storey, growing on deep alluvial soils in the central and eastern parts of the area. Light is at a premium under the extensive canopy, forcing climbing plants to 'reach for the sky' – or die. One such climber in Ngezi is *Saba cumoriensis*, a sweet-scented liana that bears white flowers and fruits that are in demand for making a popular kind of juice. There are even shrubs that in desperation also tend to climb, such as *Cossypioides kirkii*, named for the distinguished 19th-century British consul to Zanzibar. The moist forest also provides sustenance for a variety of tree ferns and orchids, as well as the **Mpapindi palm** (*Chrysulidocarpus pembanus*), endemic to Ngezi and listed among the world's endangered species. It is particularly common inland of Verani Beach.

GOING BATS ABOUT A BAT

The Pemba flying fox, as its name suggests, is unique to the island, though it isn't, of course, a fox but a large (1.7m/5.5ft across the wings) chestnut-coloured fruit bat. It is found only in moist forests, where it feeds at night on wild fruits and tree blossoms, or goes foraging for figs, mangoes and paw-paws. In doing so it helps to pollinate indigenous and exotic trees and disperse their seeds. The nocturnal bats roost (upside down) throughout the day among the canopies of big trees, often in large colonies. Because of habitat destruction and hunting (roast fruit bat was a popular dish in parts of Pemba) the species became critically endangered. Thanks to Fauna and Flora International and their local environmental partner DCCFF, and a growing enthusiasm amongst the people of Pemba, the bat has made an exciting comeback and is now estimated to number between 22,000 and 35,000 individuals. For those people who cannot get to Ngezi but are in Chake Chake there is a small flying fox sanctuary (Kidike Roost Site) just 10 minutes from that town by taxi.

Right: *Mangroves on Pemba Island. The mangrove has been exploited for years because of its termite-resistant poles, often used in construction.*

The reserve's narrow coastal fringes are covered with coral rag forest, with mangroves lining the tidal creeks. These creeks are fed by small freshwater streams as well as being washed by the tides, which at high water sweep up the streams and far into the forest, sometimes forming **brackish swamps**. In the centre of the reserve, moist forest gives way abruptly to an area of heath-land, founded on leached sand and composed of the **heather** *Philippia mafiensis*, found only on Pemba and on Mafia Island.

Ngezi has a small but extremely interesting array of wildlife, including the **Zanzibar red colobus monkey**, artificially introduced in 1970. The **Pemba vervet monkey** is also found here, and so is a subspecies of the **eastern tree hyrax**, a creature vaguely like a large, dull-coloured guinea pig but which, as its name suggests, is predominantly arboreal. Other mammals include the **Pemba blue duiker**, not much larger than a hare, **feral pigs**, descended from animals brought to Zanzibar by the Portuguese, the **marsh mongoose** (Ngezi's only mammalian carnivore) and the **Javan civet**, probably brought to Pemba by Southeast Asian traders for the musk it produces, used in the manufacture of perfumes.

Perhaps the mammal that most visitors want to see, however, is one of Ngezi's several species of bats, the

Pemba flying fox (which is described in the fact panel on page 93).

Ngezi's bird life, whilst not abundant, is diverse and in some cases – Pemba Green Pigeon (*Treron pembaensis*), Pemba Scops Owl (*Otus pembaensis*) and Pemba White-eye (*Zosterops vaughani*) – unique to the island, together with a subspecies of the Pemba African Goshawk (*Accipiter tachiro pembaensis*). Other species include the Hadada (*Bostrychia hagedash*), the Palm-nut Vulture (*Gypohierax angolensis*), the brilliantly coloured Malachite Kingfisher (*Alcedo cristata*), Broad-billed Roller (*Eurystomus glaucurus*), Crowned Hornbill (*Tockus albotenninatus*) and the Black-breasted Glossy Starling (*Lamprotornis corruscus vaughani*).

Ngezi's swamps have their own characteristic plant life. Among the trees found here is the small powder-puff tree (*Barringtonia racemosa*), the bark of which has a high tannin content, used traditionally, when ground, as an effective fish poison. Not good news for the inhabitants of the ponds found here, though the tree has its positive side (for humans at least) as it has anti-malarial properties.

Pond life includes terrapins, freshwater eels and fish of the *Tilapia* and *Claria* species, presumably introduced from the mainland many years ago. Smaller indigenous fish also thrive here, as well as a number of invertebrates, insects and worms. Needless to say, insects and other invertebrates abound throughout the entire forest and include many species of butterfly, some endemic.

Pemba's Other Forests

The most significant of Pemba's other natural forests are Ras Kiuyu in the far northeast and Msitu Kuu a little further south. **Ras Kiuyu**, because of its relatively remote location, is probably one of the least visited, least disturbed areas in Zanzibar. For adventurous travellers it represents a wonderful opportunity to explore approximately 210ha (519 acres) of dry coastal forest in almost complete isolation, and, as the forest opens on to beautiful white-sand beaches in the east, to enjoy a swim, a rock-pool walk or a picnic afterwards. The problem is in getting there, which is where the adventure comes in; without a boat it isn't easy.

IT'S A KIND OF MAGIC

A more African pursuit on Pemba is that concerned with **black (or white) magic**. It is said that 'guilds', each run by a practising master, not only flourish in Pemba but attract students of the black or white arts from all over Africa, and as far afield as Haiti. Beliefs in magic and witchcraft are widespread in sub-Saharan Africa and *waganga* (witchdoctors or traditional healers) from Pemba are seen by many Africans as being particularly skilled, and often feared, even by apparently sophisticated people; a curse from a Pemba *mganga* is not just something out of Harry Potter.

More accessible is **Msitu Kuu**, another patch (about 130ha/321 acres) of relict coastal forest to the south, close to the village of Micheweni (the Wete-Micheweni road bypasses it). Again, it is seldom visited but it is said to contain monkeys and small antelopes, as well as other forms of wildlife, including that rare endemic, the Pemba Green Pigeon.

PEMBA'S OTHER HISTORICAL SITES

As well as the fort in Chake Chake, the ruins at Ras Mkumbuu and those at Pujini, there are historical sites at **Chwaka**, in the extreme northeast of the island (15th-century ruins of two mosques, two houses and some tombs), another mosque and some tombs (probably late 17th century) at **Ras Kikokochwe** on the east coast, ruins of a medieval settlement at **Mkia wa Ng'ombe**, by the south-ern border of Ngezi Forest, and the foundations of an even older settlement on the small island of Mtambwe Mkuu in the southeast reaches of Wete harbour. The interesting thing about **Mtambwe Mkuu**, apart from the fact that former explorers apparently called it the Isle of Mystery, is that many tiny silver coins were found there in 1984, the only known example of silver coins being minted in sub-Saharan Africa (except for Kilwa) in olden times.

PEMBA'S BEACHES

Among Pemba's often small and isolated beaches are some glorious strips of white sand and blue-green seas. The fine beaches on Misali Island and Vitongoji have already been mentioned, but among the others are those on the extreme northwestern peninsula, bordering Ngezi Forest. Along the western shores of the peninsula, just south of the Ras Kigomasha lighthouse (and overlooked by the wonderfully situated Manta Reef Lodge), are **Panga ya Watoro Beach** (Machete of the Refugees), which phases into **Verani** and, after a short break in the coral rag scrub, **Tondooni**. The peninsula's eastern shoreline is blessed by the crescent-shaped **Vumawimbi** (Roaring Surf) **Beach**. All seem to have been designer-made for honeymooners, or anyone who loves sea, sand and solitude.

The far northeastern peninsula has one or two **secluded little coves** along its inland edge and a longer (3km/2-mile) beach called **Mbyuni** (Place of the Baobab) on its seaward side, just east of Ras Kiuyu Forest. At the indented tip of Kojani Island (off the east coast opposite Wete) is another lovely slip of white sand, accessible by boat from Likoni on the mainland, across from Kojani Village.

Down in the south, **Wambaa Beach** on Fundu Lagoon is the best known. It is a fairly short boat ride from Mkoani but is mostly enjoyed by the visitors to the second of Pemba's luxury lodges, the exclusive **Fundu Lagoon**. The belt of residual natural woodland behind this beach, incidentally, is superb for birders, especially if they can afford the lodge, where one can lie in bed in the pre-dawn darkness and hear the soft 'poop poop' of that highly localized endemic, the **Pemba Scops Owl**, and soon afterwards see the endemic subspecies of the **African Goshawk** in display mode high overhead. Other exciting birds in this same locality are the **Pemba White-eye** that feed around midday at the lodge (among the trees by the health spa, not in the restaurant), the diminutive **Pemba Sunbirds** (*Cinnyris pembae*) and Black-breasted Glossy Starling.

Even closer to Mkoani, 6km (4km) to the west, is a lovely 'desert island' beach on **Kwata Islet**, whilst in the extreme south are two more exquisite little beaches on a larger islet, **Shamiani**, and a third, **Kukuu**, on the nearby Ras Domoni Peninsula. There are others here and there. One day the developers will find all these places and move in but in the meantime they are yours for the asking, if you have a sense of adventure (or enough money to fly there and stay in one of the few tourist lodges).

Above: *Fundu Lagoon Resort is exclusive and luxurious.*

SUBMISSIVE SIMPLICITY

Islam means 'submission' and at the heart of Islam is submission to God. But submission to God also implies humility and the leading of a simple, rather than ostentatious or extravagant, lifestyle. Such lifestyles are common in Pemba, and the island's little towns reflect this, not merely because of poverty (which is real enough) but because of a widespread acceptance of God's will. For tourists and travellers used to relative luxuries, Pemba's simplicity can be a little stark at first, but there is a captivating tranquillity and disregard for time also, for those with the humility and patience to adapt to them, however temporarily.

Pemba at a Glance

Mid-May to mid-October, when temperatures and humidity lowest and rainfall usually minimal, though all other times of year outside the long rains (approx. mid-March to mid-May) can be enjoyable. Mid-October to mid-March can sometimes be uncomfortably hot and humid, sometimes with showers, but off-sea breezes help to counteract this and diving is at its best during this period.

GETTING THERE

Most tourists intending to visit Pemba fly first to **Dar es Salaam** or **Kilimanjaro international airports** (east and northern Tanzania) or to **Nairobi** (Kenya). Various **international airlines** cover these routes. The best option is then to fly on to Pemba using **scheduled charter flights**, directly to Pemba or via Unguja (Zanzibar Island). The most frequent route is Zanzibar to Pemba. **ZanAir** presently flies twice daily from Unguja to Pemba, **Coastal Air** once daily. There are daily flights from Dar to Pemba, mostly via Zanzibar. Similarly there are daily flights from Arusha Airport (northern Tanzania) to Pemba, again mostly via Zanzibar. Coastal Air also has a return flight each afternoon from Tanga, on the northeast Tanzanian coast, to Pemba, connecting to Zanzibar and Dar es Salaam.

Ferries do run to Pemba from Dar es Salaam and from Stone Town in Unguja but timings can be unpredictable. If you have a tight schedule in Pemba with pre-arranged bookings it is best to fly. Current air and ferry **schedules** can usually be found in one of the little local magazines, available in supermarkets, bookshops, etc. in Dar or Unguja, but even these timings need to be personally verified.

GETTING AROUND

If you have booked with one of the tourist lodges in Pemba they will tell you where to go and how, and probably pick you up at some point. Otherwise it's a question of finding a taxi or going around on an often crowded *dala-dala* (local bus). Or of course hiring a bike. Boat trips to various tourist attractions (such as Misali Island) for sightseeing/ diving/snorkelling/picnicking, etc. can usually be arranged from Chake Chake, Mkoani or Wete or from one of the lodges/resorts.

WHERE TO STAY

Accommodation in Pemba, other than at the few tourist-class resorts, is usually in the form of basic guesthouses or small hotels, and meals, once they arrive, can fall somewhat short of 'exciting'. But if you enjoy travelling, these places can be enjoyable in a some-times perverse way.

Mkoani

Not many non-locals stay in Mkoani but the best option is perhaps the **Jondeni Guesthouse**, tel: (0)24 245 6042, on the hilltop 1km (0.6 miles) north of the port. Simple but pleasant enough, offering various boat trips and snorkelling excursions.

Chake Chake
BUDGET
Mamy Hotel and Restaurant, tel: (0)777 432 789. A little out of town (at Machomane) but clean and friendly guesthouse, worth considering. **Pemba Island Hotel**, tel: (0)24 245 2215. Clean and reasonable.

Wete
MID-RANGE TO BUDGET
Pemba Crown Hotel, tel: (0)24 245 2660, www.pemba crown.com Opposite market. Clean and good value though no restaurant. **Treasure Island Hotel**, tel: (0)24 245 4171. Large, new high-rise place 2km (1 mile) from town centre. Rooms clean, comfortable and quite big, with a rooftop terrace.

BUDGET
Bomani Guesthouse, tel: (0)24 245 4384. Close to market. Laid-back, friendly. **Sharook Guesthouse**, tel: (0)24 245 4386, tel: (0)777 431 012. Centre of town, owned by helpful local family. Rooms quite spacious.

Pemba at a Glance

Dive Lodges/Resorts
LUXURY

Fundu Lagoon Resort, tel (reservations): +255 (0)76 35 92 820; email (reservations): info.@fundulagoon.com www.fundulagoon.com
'Barefoot luxury' is a phrase much in vogue with regard to resorts like this, and 'in vogue' is appropriate as Fundu Lagoon has acquired good write-ups from some of the 'posher' magazines. Fine location on Wambaa Beach in southwest Pemba, wonderful place for diving, honeymooning or birding. All the facilities and services one might expect of an exclusive luxury resort.

Manta Reef Lodge, tel: (0)777 423 930, www.mantareef lodge.com Manta Reef is situated in one of the best locations in Zanzibar, on Panga ya Watoro Beach in the extreme northwest of the island. It isn't cheap but is delightfully low-key, excellent for divers, snorkellers or naturalists (with a wealth of marine life on one side and the endemic wonders of Ngezi Forest on the other) or, of course, for honeymooners who also dive.

MID-RANGE TO BUDGET

Kervan Saray, tel: (0)773 176 737/8 (let it ring out at least three times!). This refreshingly unpretentious lodge, in the words of its engagingly eccentric co-owner/manager Raf Jah, is 'a dive shop with

rooms', located on the long beach just west of Makangale Village in Pemba's extreme northwest, close to some of the best dive sites in the world, as a resort run by the highly experienced Swahili Divers would be. And close to endemic-rich Ngezi Forest. 'Turkish Raf' and his wife Francisca have operated in Pemba since 1999 and claim 'a collection of Pemba firsts: first PADI resort, BSAC resort, PADI five-star resort and the first hotel to use RIBS'. Whatever that is. Oh, and Pemba's first resort swimming pool, though don't expect landscaped infinity. Diving and diving safety are taken seriously (no wild descents into the fathomless depths here, unless you convince Raf that you are a true expert, when he might lend you his Pony cylinder). Rooms are big, dive kit new, premises basic, atmosphere warm and welcoming.

If you are staying in a tourist resort (or on a live-aboard) you eat there and you eat well. Otherwise in Pemba you pays your money and you takes your choice, which isn't all that extensive…

Pemba isn't geared for tourism except for the few lodges and resorts so you have to be a bit creative

and/or ask around. Excursions to **Ngezi Forest** are organized by the resorts in that area, and perhaps from local operators in Wete or Chake Chake. Trips to certain **beaches** or ruins (such as **Pujini**) are also possible from Chake Chake. Resorts within striking distance of **Misali Island** will take you there for **diving/ snorkelling/swimming/nature walks**, etc., as well as to various **dive sites**, and you can also hire boats in Chake Chake to take you to the **Quanbalu Ruins** and Misali. Outings to '**bullfights**' might be possible from Chake Chake or Mkoani in the season. There are now spice tours in Pemba as well as Unguja. Ask in your hotel or at Jambo Tours (Chake Chake). Also, close to Chake Chake there is a Flying Fox Reserve and an Essential Oils Factory. Again, ask at your hotel or Jambo Tours.

Chake Chake
Airline Tickets: Coastal Aviation, tel: (0)777 418 343; ZanAir tel: (0)24 245 2990, tel: (0)777 420 760.
Jambo Tours & Safaris: tel: (0)777 437 397/468 809.
Hospitals: Chake Chake (not recommended except in emergencies), tel: (0)24 245 2311.
Public Health Lab: diagnostic tests, tel: (0)24 245 2473.

7. The Other Zanzibar: Beneath the Sea

In the past tourists and travellers were drawn to the isles mainly by the history of Stone Town and Unguja's beautiful beaches, but an increasing number of people have begun to explore the other Zanzibar, beneath the sea. As this shift in emphasis takes place, Pemba, long neglected, is beginning to be seen as a place of great tourism potential.

The dive sites in Pemba and Unguja are now recognized as being among the best in the Indian Ocean, if not the world, as are some of their snorkelling and game-fishing areas. More and more resorts are catering for, or specializing in, such activities, and more and more people are enjoying the thrills and wonders of the world beneath the waves.

SNORKELLING

There are some excellent snorkelling sites around Zanzibar. Among the best are Mnemba Atoll and Chumbe Island (Unguja), and Misali Island (Pemba) but there are many others, including Tumbatu Island (off northwest Unguja). Learning to **snorkel** is reasonably straightforward, though it can take a bit of getting used to and sometimes be a little unnerving. You are, after all, out of your natural element, and learning to breathe through a snorkel tube and swim with fins are also unnatural. But you will get the hang of it if you persevere, and pretty soon the excitement of being (and seeing) underwater will override any initial anxieties.

However, common sense dictates that you **consult local experts** and keep to the safe sites, in the still-water lagoons and pools, until you are more experienced. **Tide surges and strong, sometimes unpredictable currents** can

DON'T MISS

★★★ **Diving** (if you are experienced) one of the more outstanding sites.
★★★ Diving/snorkelling at **Mnemba Island** (Unguja) or **Misali** (Pemba), experienced or beginner.
★★★ Learning to dive/snorkel.
★★★ **Big-game fishing** if that's your kind of sport.

Opposite: *A diver looking at the remnants of the* Paraportiani, *off southern Pemba.*

Above: *Divers getting ready for a dive.*

be dangerous. Unguja, with its shallower, often calmer waters, its peaceful lagoons and their adjacent reefs, is often ideal for snorkelling, which is normally best attempted on an **incoming tide**, as outgoing waters often stir up sand and other sediments.

Scuba Diving
The Practicalities of Diving in Zanzibar
Pemba generally offers more challenging diving than Unguja and is rated highly by experienced divers (which does not mean that Pemba is off limits for beginners or that experts won't enjoy diving in Unguja).

Scuba diving is not as difficult as many people think. You do not need to be an Olympic swimmer, only to be able to swim a minimum of 200m (219yd) in your own way and time and to tread water or float for 10 minutes. Children aged 12 and above can learn and so can senior citizens, and very few medical complaints will debar you from scuba diving; ask a reputable company in your own country or in Zanzibar for advice.

The world's largest and most respected recreational dive-training organization is **PADI** (Professional Association of Diving Instructors). You will see the initials PADI on most, if not all, of the dive company signs and ads throughout Zanzibar. This is an indication that the company embraces and maintains high PADI standards and runs properly accredited courses.

Such courses typically begin with 'Discover Scuba Dive' and 'Scuba Diver' through more advanced, more expensive courses to 'Dive Master'. Fees vary but one company in Nungwi, in 2009, was charging US$95 for the 'Discover Scuba', US$330 for 'Scuba Diver' and US$480 for 'Open Water'. Actual dive packages (including use of equipment) also vary but this particular operator was asking US$60 for a single local dive, US$190 for a four-dive package, US$280 for a six-dive package and US$400 for a ten-dive package.

A snorkelling trip might cost you about US$20 (half-day to a nearby site, not including lunch) to about US$50 for a trip (including lunch) to a prime site in the area, such as Mnemba Island. Equipment rental for mask, fins and snorkel is around US$10 per person per outing. These fees are only a rough-and-ready guide and will obviously change; anyone interested should check current rates, preferably before their journey to Zanzibar, by contacting resorts or companies via the Internet (or later in person).

What Might You See?

Despite the enthralling possibilities, visitors occasionally find the diving in Zanzibar less exciting than expected. Much depends on where you go, and when, and with whom. Some people come with unrealistic expectations, hoping to see whales, sharks, whale sharks, dolphins, etc. on every outing (or at least on one), but the Indian Ocean is not an aquarium, any more than the East African bush is a zoo. If you are lucky count your blessings; if not, what better reason to come back to Zanzibar?

Be assured, however, that the big fellows are out there. Humpback whales are seen at the surface fairly often (mostly in September/October). Indo-Pacific bottlenose, humpback and spinner dolphins might also be seen in various places (the bottlenose is almost guaranteed on the dolphin tours from Kizimkazi, where several pods – up

---

HOW DANGEROUS IS DIVING?

Scuba diving is sometimes said to be one of the world's most dangerous sports but diving, like mountaineering, has various levels of difficulty and danger. It will always involve a certain risk, otherwise there would be little adventure or sense of accomplishment, but risks are minimal if you are properly trained and equipped, responsible, aware of what is going on around you and respectful of the sea. And if you choose a dive centre with a good reputation and safety record.

PAPA SHILINGI

The whale shark is sometimes known in Swahili as *Papa Shilingi*, the spots on its back said to be shillings showered upon the prototype by God. The largest living fish, it grows to over 12m (almost 40ft) and weighs 13.6 tonnes (15 tons). Its mouth, 1.5m (5ft) wide, is filled with more than 300 rows of tiny teeth. Despite all this, it is a filter feeder and poses no danger to divers except perhaps from an accidental swish of its tail. It can live for 70 years, originated about 60 million years ago and can dive to depths of over 700m (2300ft).

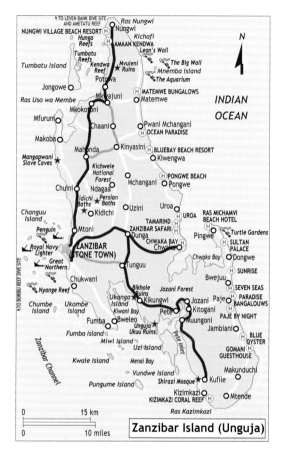

Zanzibar Island (Unguja)

to 150 strong – are resident. Whale sharks are also seen fairly frequently (usually in August/September or January/February) but you need some luck. Other sharks, notably black- or white-tipped reef sharks and at some sites hammerheads and tiger, also occur. Various rays are present, though the iconic manta is pelagic and migratory and therefore relatively unpredictable (January is said to be the best time). Green turtles, which nest in suitable places around the archipelago, are quite common, hawksbill (which also nest in the archipelago) are less plentiful but still frequently observed.

The larger pelagics (including big game fish) materialize out of the blue unannounced (and sometimes unobserved, as you will be constantly distracted by the abundance of reef fishes and other creatures that live in and around the fantastic coral gardens and precipitous walls). Dive in the right frame of mind and you will rarely be disappointed.

A Dive Site by any other Name...

Most major dive sites and some of the best snorkelling areas in Unguja and Pemba are listed below but new sites are being discovered all the time and given a name by the centre involved, resulting in some confusion as other centres come along and often give it a completely different name. Dive centres also often have a cluster of sites in the same area, which compounds the confusion. Every effort has been made here to achieve uniformity but it hasn't been easy or completely successful and in a constantly changing situation some inconsistencies are inevitable. Visitors should not worry about this as the centres they choose will have their own established names and the better operators know their sites intimately.

DIVING AND SNORKELLING SITES AROUND UNGUJA

The dive scene in Unguja is quite complex. While it cannot generally compete with some of Pemba's world-class sites it nevertheless boasts some excellent blue water dives with many exquisite corals. It also has a range of standard reefs that might not get the adrenalin pumping through the veins of more experienced divers but which add immensely to the enjoyment of your beach holiday. It also has some 'muck dive' sites, as the experts know them, which might have very low visibility but which also host a wealth of incredible macro life ('the weird stuff' as one diver has called it). As with diving elsewhere, much depends on the guide that you have and the company you go with. There are about 20 or more dive sites around the north of Unguja but within these 20 are some specific areas. Sites in each area are listed in alphabetical order. Any 'K' ratings refer to the star system (zero to five) adopted by the respected diving expert Anton Koornhof.

Stone Town

Stone Town has some surprisingly good dive sites, including several wrecks, and a couple of dives in the area would add greatly to any diver's Zanzibar experience. Experienced divers could expect to get at least four days of satisfying diving off Stone Town, especially if diving with one of the top operators such as One Ocean.

Bawe Island: Six kilometres (4 miles) west of Stone Town, with a 'K' rating of four stars for diving, three for snorkelling, maximum depth 18m (59ft). Reef encircles islet, sloping up from sandy bed with overhangs and occasional pinnacles. Known for beautiful corals, including brain and staghorn, and large, varied populations of reef fishes. Moray eels,

---

CORALS

Corals are tiny creatures called polyps, related to sea anemones, which they resemble. Each coral forms a cup-like shell of limestone around itself in lieu of a skeleton. As the polyps develop they divide and form colonies, which gradually build up one on top of the other to create coral reefs. Specific colonies may be up to 1000 years old, and coral reefs many thousands, forming slowly and responding to changes in sea level and other environmental conditions.

DOUBLE TROUBLE

Next time you find yourself staring into the rather daunting jaws of a moray eel as it surveys you balefully from a coral crevice, be grateful you are not one of its prey species, for after seizing some poor victim in its jaws, a second set of jaws (known as pharyngeal) reaches forward from the moray's throat, grabs the prey and carries it back to the esophagus for swallowing.

Above: *A juvenile clown fish among the tentacles of an anemone.*

UNDERWATER PARROTS

Parrotfish are often as colourful as parrots themselves, though the name is derived from the fishes' tightly packed teeth, which form a parrot-like bill. This is used for rasping algae from coral, etc., a process that (through the calcified droppings of countless parrotfish over the centuries) helps to create Zanzibar's gloriously white beaches. At night parrotfish squeeze into crevices, some species secreting a thick coat of mucus that might mask their scent from moray eels and other nocturnal predators.

octopuses and puffer fish are sometimes seen.

Boribu Reef: Advanced divers only and 45 minutes from Stone Town even by fast boat but a fine dive site ('K' rating four for diving, zero for snorkelling). Its reef, descending to around 30m (98ft), sustains fascinating coral formations, including spectacular columna, gorgonian fans, honeycombs, and huge barrel sponges. Large pelagics such as barracuda and tuna might be seen, as well as morays and big lobsters. Whale sharks sometimes encountered.

Changuu (Prison Island): Good snorkelling 35m (115ft) northwest of the main beach.

Chapwani Island (Grave Island): Good snorkelling 50m (164ft) northwest of eastern tip.

Chumbe Island: One of the best shallow water reefs in the world. Scuba diving not allowed within the sanctuary but snorkelling superb. The reef crest, with its fantastic array of hard corals, is only 1–3m (3–10ft) below the surface, depending on the state of the tide, giving snorkellers access to an underwater world normally only accessible to scuba divers. A world populated by almost 400 species of fish, including angel, barracuda, bat, blue-spotted stingrays, box, butterfly, lion, parrot, trigger, trumpet, and unicorn, as well as sweetlips and Moorish idols. You might even see a dolphin, a resident hawksbill turtle or lobsters.

Great Northern (wreck): This cable layer sank (one can't help wondering what the crew had been up to) on New Year's Eve 1902. Every cloud has its silver lining, however, and the wreck has been transformed by corals and other marine organisms into a home for geometric moray eels, lionfish and many leaf fish, among others. The ship's hull is broken in two but parts of the vessel are still recognizable. At a maximum depth of 16m (52ft) and with normally excellent visibility, it is said to be ideal for novice divers and excellent for snorkellers. Lies just southwest of Pange Island.

Murogo: Sandbar, 35 minutes by boat west of Stone Town. The sloping reef, with depths from 3m (10ft) to about 24m (79ft), makes Murogo suitable for newcomers to open-water diving, as well as more advanced divers, with overhangs and swim-throughs enhancing the experience. 'K' rating of five for diving, three for snorkelling and said to be good place to see turtles, blue-spotted stingrays, puffer and anemone fish, as well as a magnificent array of brain, plate and staghorn corals.

Nyange Reef: Largest of the west coast reefs, off Nyange sandbank just southwest of Stone Town. 'K' rating of four for diving and for snorkelling, maximum depth 26m (85ft). At least three important dive sites are to be found here, Coral Bay, Groupers' Playground and Turtles' Den, their names self-explanatory. Large variety of reef fish and apparently an endemic species of coral.

Pange Island: Sandbar just off Stone Town, with a 'K' rating of three for diving and for snorkelling, maximum depth 14m (46ft). Said to be ideal for open-water dive courses as site is calm and shallow. An extensive range of corals and reef fish to be seen, including clownfish, Moorish idols and parrotfish. Reef is also suitable for night dives, during which crabs, cuttlefish and squid might be seen.

Penguin (wreck): Remains of steam-driven sand-dredger *Penguin*, just north of Pange Island, a short boat ride from Stone Town. Reserved for experienced divers, depths to 40m (131ft). Attracts large numbers of barracuda, bluefin trevally, morays, large stingrays and many others.

Royal Navy Lighter (wreck): Advanced divers only. The remains of this mid-20th-century wreck, covered in whip

THE *HMS PEGASUS*

World War I, bitterly contested as the Ice Cream War on the mainland, hardly involved Zanzibar directly. However, soon after the war broke out the German light cruiser *Koenigsberg* sneaked into Zanzibar waters and sank the British cruiser *HMS Pegasus* as she lay at anchor off Shangani Point, with a loss of 38 lives. The *Koenigsberg* was later crippled by the Royal Navy in the Rufiji Delta and scuttled by her captain. There is little to be seen of the *HMS Pegasus*. She was sold for scrap in 1955, blasted open by dynamite and everything of value removed.

Above: *'In an octopus's garden by the sea'. A large octopus sits on a coral surrounded by fish.*

NAPOLEON – OR COULD IT BE JOSEPHINE?

The Napoleon wrasse is one of the largest reef fishes in the world (some grow to over 2m/6.5ft), yet it is a gentle, almost affectionate giant with surprisingly expressive eyes, like something from an animated cartoon. It often approaches divers, sometimes even nudging them as if wanting to be petted. The hump on its head is said to resemble a Napoleon-style hat. Adult females sometimes change sex; no one (least of all, you can bet, the confused males) knows why.

---

and other corals, are situated at around 30m (98ft), just south of Bawe Island and about 20 minutes from Stone Town. Possible sightings include barracuda, bluefin, cobia, fusiliers, guinea fowl blaasops, Jewfish, morays, rainbow runners, silver sweetlips, large stingrays, sweepers, trevally and yellow-finned goatfish. Reef sharks sometimes encountered.

Kendwa/Nungwi

Ametatu Reef: Entry-level site about 15 minutes or so offshore, northeastern headland, depths of about 14m (46ft). Good beginners' dive with many reef fish among the corals.

Hunga Reefs: Superb dive site, a four-in-one cluster of coral bommies (coral outcrops) a short boat ride from Kendwa. Hunga has a variety of hard, soft and fan corals, with depths of about 12–18m (39–59ft). Said to be a beautiful open-water site for experienced divers and densely populated with fish, including the occasional shoal of barracudas and perhaps a reef shark. Other welcome distractions include slow-moving but often extravagantly coloured nudibranches, shrimps and various species of reef fishes, among them batfish, crocodile fish, Moorish idols, scorpionfish, stonefish, large schools of surgeon- and unicornfish and great numbers of yellow sweetlips, as well as Napoleons and blue-spotted rays. Can only be dived on specific tides.

Kendwa Reef: Easily accessible from Kendwa Beach, offering several sites suitable for novices and more experienced divers. Among the best sites is **Mbwangawa** (maximum depth 18m/59ft), a long, extensive slope covered in cabbage corals with many yellow sweetlips in attendance. Another lovely site is the **Kendwa Coral Garden**, known for its corals and reef fish. Depths of only 3–8m (10–26ft) make it suitable for snorkelling as well as scuba-diving novices or more experienced divers.

Leven Bank: Exciting dive, experienced divers only as there are dangerously strong currents and considerable depths. Large, coral-covered plateau, about 7km (4 miles) wide, 14km (9 miles) north of Ras Nungwi. Depths vary but plateau slopes down to about 40m (131ft) then drops abruptly to about 200m (656ft) in the east and 80m (262ft) to the west. 'K' rating of five (diving) with great variety of corals, including clusters of honeycomb and pillar, and funnel sponges 'as big as dustbins'. Large schools of reef fish, barracuda, groupers, guitarfish, kingfish, huge moray eels and very large Napoleons, though sadly some of the larger pelagics have been fished out. Manta rays and whale sharks might be seen at certain seasons.

Nankivell Rock: Another of Unguja's top dive sites. Large clump of corals (including impressive brain, plate and devil's whip) surrounded by sand, between Kendwa and northern tip of **Tumbatu Island**. Depths are between 14 and 20m (46–66ft). Good site for novices to practise drift diving, though only on certain tides. Lots of game fish, occasional small reef sharks and a wide range of reef fishes, as well as lobsters, can be seen here.

Tumbatu Reefs: The muck diving (as the connoisseurs call it) off Tumbatu is for experienced divers who want to see an incredible array of macro life. Sea horses, eels, leaf fish, frog fish and nudibranches abound here, and there are some wonderful corals. The dives are fairly flat at 18m (59ft) but do slope down towards 24m (79ft). Sometimes you might find yourself diving in a current but it is well worth any inconvenience. Intermediate divers may also enjoy this site, but need to be warned that the visibility can be pretty bad.

Nungwi/Matemwe

Kichafi: Circular lagoon just off the northeastern Nungwi Peninsula. Probably best barrier reef site (Mnemba excepted) in this vicinity, depths of 8–18m (26–59ft). Plate, lettuce leaf sheet and staghorn coral, ideal site for underwater photography and night dives (including beginners). Abundance of underwater life such as turtles, schools of

---

FLAPJACK FLAMENCO

Imagine a misshapen red-and-white pancake doing the flamenco underwater and you might appreciate why scuba divers sometimes flutter their fins in excitement about what are generically known as sea slugs. The Spanish dancer is actually the largest (up to 20cm) of a group of marine gastropods known as nudi-branches, many flamboyantly coloured. Like the ladies it is named after, it is usually encountered at night. It dances silently, however, not to the strum of guitars or the clack of castanets.

Above: *The colourful nudibranch* Chromodoris geminus.

black and blue-lined snappers, crocodile fish, blue-spotted stingrays, Napoleons, parrotfish, moray eels, snappers, marbled groupers, oriental sweetlips, wrasse, and colourful nudibranches. Octopuses, lobsters and crabs emerge by night, as the parrotfish doze (we are told) 'in their mucous sleeping bags'.

Chaka Tuni Reef: A little way northeast of Nungwi lighthouse, depths of around 8–18m (26–59ft), accessible to all categories of divers. Composed of plate and big pavona corals. Marine life includes many green turtles, angel- and butterflyfish, blue-spotted rays, moray eels and lobsters.

Kombe: Steeply leaning wall ranging from 7–8m (23–59ft), with a further drop-off to 35m (115ft), north of Matemwe on Unguja's fringing reef. Suitable for all levels of divers, with a fine bed of foliose coral, complete with sponges and anemones, and a wealth of marine life, including small blue-spotted ribbontail rays, lionfish and, in the many holes in the wall, lobsters and mantis shrimps. Dolphins are possible, as are guitarfish and reef sharks. Visibility might be limited in windy conditions.

Leon's Wall: Just off east coast of Nungwi Peninsula and northwest of Mnemba Island. Said to be suitable for novices, as well as more advanced divers, with depths of around 5–30m (16–98ft). Upper regions appropriate for snorkellers whilst the wall gives divers the chance to explore its overhangs and caves. A variety of corals flourish here, including big gorgonian sea fans. Fish species might include large bass, leaf fish, lionfish and snappers. Big game fish sometimes sighted, as are dolphins and sharks, whilst in September or early October humpback whales are occasionally observed at the surface.

BILLFISH

Six species of billfish (those with swordfish-like extended bills) occur around Zanzibar. Of the three marlins among them, the longest is the blue (though in East Africa the black might be generally heavier), the most numerous and colourful the striped. The broadbill is said to be the toughest billfish to catch, and the sailfish is perhaps the most visibly spectacular because of its great dorsal fin. The shortbill spearfish is rarely caught or even seen.

Mnemba Island

Unguja's premier diving/snorkelling area with many (sometimes crowded) sites. Reefs easily accessible and many nearby resorts have dive centres. Visibility can drop to around 10m (33ft) in July/August and is at its best in January. Sea conditions best around October/November.

The Aquarium: Appropriately named, depths of 16–25m (52–82ft). Initial sector suitable for beginners with spread of shallow-lying coral bommies across sandy bed. Photographic opportunities abound as there are some beautiful corals, hard and soft, and sponges, and a kaleidoscope of reef fishes. Lower down the slope (15–25m/49–82ft) is a wonderland of foliose coral, home to lots of large jacks and groupers. This phases into another sweep of sand and scattered bommies, good for blue-spotted ribbontail rays and occasional reef sharks. Green and hawksbill turtles sometimes seen.

The Big Wall: One of Zanzibar's best dive sites, northeastern corner of Mnemba Atoll, with depths of between 12m (39ft) and well over 60m (197ft). This 1km (0.6-mile) long reef is for experienced divers only, when tides are favourable and waters calm. Visibility normally excellent (over 40m/131ft). After a rapid descent to 30m (98ft) divers find themselves alongside the precipitous wall, with its many interesting overhangs, but one eye should be kept open, as you drift-dive along, for large pelagics emerging from 'the blue'. Giant barracudas, bluefin trevally, Napoleons, rays (bluespotted eagles often seen), rainbow runners, reef sharks, tuna and sometimes dolphinfish are possible. Dolphins themselves frequently appear, as (less often) do whale sharks (mostly August/ November and February).

Coral Garden: Just northwest of Mnemba Island, depths from 5–40m (16–131ft). Experienced

SUBMARINE STEALTH BOMBER

The manta ray, with its diamond-shaped body, black above and white below, looks like a stealth bomber but is peacefully intentioned and more graceful, though it 'flies' through the water (and occasionally, and briefly, above it). The largest known specimen was around 7.6m (25ft) across. Mantas are filter feeders, cruising the oceans and along the reefs taking in plankton, fish larvae, etc., and sometimes visiting 'cleaning stations' where small fishes feed inside its gills and over its body, removing parasites in the process.

Below: *A diver off Mnemba Island. Divers are encouraged to dive with a 'buddy'.*

divers only. Wide range of beautiful corals, particularly big fan formations, as well as many species of reef fish, garden and snowflake eels and sometimes big game fish, barracuda and kingfish. Turtles regularly sighted.

Kichwani: Steep coral bank, depths from 20–40m (65–131ft). Beyond 30m (98ft) is a vertical wall, excellent for drift-diving. Lots of healthy corals, including brain, fan, honeycomb, mushroom and staghorn. Dolphins commonly seen during boat trips or on site, which is populated by a wide range of fish species, some in large shoals. Among them are groupers, large schools of big-eyed jacks, morays, rudderfish, five-lined snappers, sweetlips, trumpetfish, wrasse and sometimes reef sharks and manta rays. Corals said to 'swarm with anthias' and often large Napoleon wrasse or other pelagic game fish 'patrol the deep'.

East of Kichwani is a pleasant coral garden, **Sinawi**, in the form of a shallow slope ranging from 5–12m (16–39ft). Turtles might be observed here and there are plenty of batfish, morays and sea slugs.

Pungu Wall: Little-visited site east of Mnemba. It can be quite exciting but is limited to experienced divers and weather conditions must be carefully respected. The dive starts with free descent to 35m (115ft) when you swim along the brim of a wall that falls off to 70m (230ft). Corals are scarce but because of the deep water beyond the wall you might encounter barracuda, eagle rays, large groupers (up to 2.5m/8ft), schools of big jacks, sharks and tuna, as well as turtles.

Wattabomi: Attractive coral gardens south of Mnemba Island, suitable for beginners or more advanced divers, depths from 12–25m (39–82ft) and gentle currents. It is claimed that you might bump into the odd whale here (metaphorically speaking) but you are much more likely to see turtles (green or hawksbill) or dolphins, not to mention a profusion of fish species including barracudas, black snappers, blue-spotted rays, blue-streak, cleaner wrasse, leaf fish, marbled groupers, peppered moray eels, powder-blue surgeonfish, regal angelfish and red-tooth triggers. Flounders and soles bury themselves in the sandy areas of the sea bed.

Paje/Jambiani

The southeast coast, despite being only an hour or so from Stone Town, is still low-key in terms of tourism. The more exposed nature of the east coast is sometimes a disadvantage with regard to diving and snorkelling but there are some very good sites within and beyond the barrier reef. As the reef from Kizimkazi almost to Paje is in the form of a wall, sightings of dolphins are always possible. New sites are being discovered all the time, though only a few are mentioned here.

Barracuda Point: This extensive coral garden with its bommies and overhangs harbours various reef fishes and shellfish. Dive begins by following slope of the bed down to around 25m (82ft).

Big Cave (Groupers' Grotto): Dive of moderate difficulty, good for drift-diving. Usually conducted by dropping alongside the wall (10–35m/32–115ft) that leads to the cave and finishing up in a coral garden. Site known for its big groupers, barracudas, large morays, and sizeable lobsters, in addition to beautiful corals and many species of reef fish. Large rays and reef sharks also possible, and when current is running masses of fish schooling and feeding near the surface.

Above: *Starry Moray Eel hiding among the corals.*

GAME-FISHING PROFILES: BLACK MARLIN

Qualities: A very powerful performer and voracious feeder, known for its long runs and 'tail-walking'. Relatively short but heavily bodied (black marlin over 900kg/1985lb have been caught off East Africa by commercial fishermen).
Best times to catch: August to October inclusive.

SMALLER GAME FISH

Giant trevally: Common in most waters as they seem to be highly territorial and often sedentary around the reef drop-offs. Fine sporting fish noted for its size and strength.

Kingfish: Highly mobile, hard-running species that often dives deep and sometimes leaps high.

Dorado: Another name for the dolphinfish (not a dolphin!). Found in the deep blue as well as close to the coast. Hooked dorado may leap or tail-walk, darting one way then the other, sometimes at great speed.

Wahoo: A member of the mackerel family, the wahoo has very sharp teeth and a high turn of speed, sometimes racing out several hundred metres of line in seconds. Often shakes its head violently in an attempt to dislodge the hook.

Barracuda: Barracuda occur offshore and around the reefs, predominantly at or near the surface. The larger ones are almost invariably loners. Often strike savagely and frequently jump out of water when hooked.

Jambiani Reef: Situated offshore from Jambiani Village. 'K' rating of four for diving, zero for snorkeling. Known for its fine array of corals. Jambiani Canyon, part of this reef, is said to be a beautiful site with a rich array of marine life, including beautiful corals, and suitable for night diving. Depths are up to 15m (49ft).

Stingray Alley: Within the lagoon just offshore from Jambiani Village. 'K' rating of four stars for diving, zero for snorkelling. Name inspired by the large numbers of blue-spotted and flap-nosed rays that you might see here. Said to be an easy dive with depths to around 18m (59ft). Visibility sometimes poor in June/July because of southerly winds.

Sau Inn Garden: Delightful garden of assorted, beautifully coloured corals and many species of fish. Depths reach around 20m (66ft).

Turtle Garden: Just off Paje. Thanks to the barrel sponges found here (favourites with turtles) this site is appropriately named. The sponges also attract large eels.

Kizimkazi

Lionfish and Jackfish Wall: Off the southern tip of Unguja in the so-called 'dolphins' playground', the dolphins in question being bottlenose and humpback. Depths of around 25m (82ft).

DIVING AND SNORKELLING SITES AROUND PEMBA

Diving in Pemba is characterized by exceptionally clear, blue water drop-offs and vibrantly healthy shallow reefs, though strong currents are common. The best option for snorkellers is Misali Island.

Northwest Pemba

Atatürk's Wall: Named presumably by 'Turkish Raf' of Swahili Divers, this site, off Uvinje Island, is 'a steep slope that goes on for ever'. Sharks, barracuda and kingfish have all been seen along the lush reef that is often best viewed at 15m (49ft) depth or less. Suitable for all divers.

The Cave: Upper part of this reef has a shallow (4m/13ft) sandy bottom, falling away abruptly in a sheer cliff to more than 100m (328ft). Cave itself situated on this wall.

Large pelagics always around and turtles possible along coral cliff, but currents can be strong.

Eggers Ascent: Sloping reef south of Trigger corner, said to host 'simply stunning marine life'. Suitable for all divers.

Emilio's Passage/The Crack: Ignoring Swahili Divers' rather suggestive label, which Manta Reef's name, The Crack, does little to redeem, we can safely say that the cleft in question is that between Njao and Fundo islands, off Pemba's main northwest coast, said to have been created by the parting of tectonic plates that form the earth's crust and apparently clearly visible to divers.

Pemba Island

Fundo Express/Deep Freeze:
Immediately west of gap between Fundo and Njao islands, with large sheer walls incorporating many overhangs and caverns. Visibility from 20–40m (66–131ft). Corals particularly attractive, especially the large rose coral and red and yellow sea fans. Fish species abundant. Experienced divers only due to possibility of strong currents.

The Gauntlet: 'An exhilarating dive' situated between Ras Ukunjwi and Fundo Island, best attempted on incoming tide from the top end of the reef (around 10m/33ft). After over-swimming a series of pretty coral bommies you can then proceed downwards to 25m (82ft) to the top of the Gauntlet's wall, from where you will be swept quickly across the void that gives this site its name. Interesting overhangs and rock formations caused by deep fissures in cliff face.

**GAME-FISHING PROFILES:
SHORTBILL SPEARFISH**

Qualities: Rarely encountered, highly migratory deep-water species feeding at or near the surface on medium-sized fish. Another light-tackle species.
Best times to catch: Mid-November to March inclusive, December best of all.

Qualities: More streamlined than the shorter black, with a long slender bill and particularly fast take-off speed. Fights aggressively and athletically when hooked, often clearing the water and running hard and long, sometimes diving deep to conserve energy.
Best times to catch: August to October inclusive, when they tend to be heavier after feasting on tuna.

Mandela/DF Malan's Wall: Named 'Mandela' by Manta Reef divers, who discovered it on the day that Nelson Mandela was released from prison, this site lies just off the southwestern edge of Njao Island. The top of this wall is between 8 and 15m (26–49ft) deep, dropping precipitously in places to more than 200m (656ft), adorned with gorgonian sea fans and whip corals. This breathtaking site provides four dives in one, including the often entrancing shallow reef along the top of the wall. Large 'blue water' species such as manta rays might occasionally be encountered.

Manta Point: One of the world's finest dive sites, off the southwestern edge of Njao Island, though mantas now said to be rare. Main feature a spectacular coral pinnacle rising from about 800m (2625ft) to around 6m (29ft) of the surface, flocculent with fantastic cabbage and other corals, with dramatic drop on its western side. Visibility varies from about 20 to 40m (66–131ft). Whole range of marine life, from fusiliers, jackfish and surgeonfish to reef sharks and turtles might be seen here, where according to one expert you would need to do ten dives back-to-back to exhaust the possibilities. Experienced divers only when currents are running strong though said to be available to all divers in quiet conditions.

Below: *Table corals and reef fishes on a submarine mountain off Pemba.*

Njao Gap: Just off northwest tip of Njao Island. Interesting, dramatic dive for experienced divers as the lovely coral garden that slopes from 5 to 18m (16–59ft) suddenly plummets into 'undiveable depths' and currents can be strong. Best drift-dived, allowing northerly current to sweep you through the gap into the lagoon beyond, without risk of getting lost. Vertical walls, giant sea fans, mantas, green and hawksbill turtles, large Napoleon wrasse and a host of titan trigger fish make this site memorable. Visibility usually excellent.

Rudi's Wall: Small deep wall on north side of the Njao Gap that always has emperors and groupers and some jacks at 30m (98ft). One of Pemba's most interesting dive sites in good visibility. Advanced divers only.

Slobodan's Bunker: Another of Swahili Divers' enigmatically named sites, this (said to be 'semi-secret') is in the form of a series of 'fingers' near Kashani Island that are full of the most prolific marine life. Advanced divers only.

Swiss Reef/Lighthouse/Shimba Hills: Three distinct sites just off extreme northwestern tip of Pemba, but close enough together to be treated as one. Gentle wall with multitude of fish, among them mantas, Napoleons, trevally and occasionally hammerheads. If current running hard, for experienced divers only, depths to 30m (98ft).

Trigger Corner: Covers entire south side of the Njao Gap. In the form of a wall that can, given good visibility and if dropped on the corner itself, be one of Pemba's most dramatic. Has a vibrant reef on top. Said to be suitable for all if accompanied by a professional guide.

West Pemba

Devil's Wall: Steep dramatic wall off Kashani Island. Once dived by many companies but now only visited occasionally, which is a pity as it is a fine and serene site.

Kokota Reef: Just off the tip of Ras Fuini on mid-western coast. Said to be ideal for night diving as waters are shallow and generally calm, ranging between 8 and 20m (26–66ft). Among creatures to be seen here, if you are lucky, is that remarkable nudibranch the Spanish dancer.

Misali Island: All the following sites in this section (West Pemba) are around Misali, except for the last, Murray's Wall. Misali, 18km (11 miles) west of Chake Chake, is a relatively accessible and popular island ('popular' in Pemba being far from crowded) and, like Mnemba in Unguja, superb for snorkelling and diving. Visibility apparently averages between 40 and 50m (131–164ft).

Big Blue: Deep-water dive during which you drift along Misali's southern channel. It is said that 'you need eyes in the back of your head for this dive as the possibility of reef sharks, barracuda and giant rays is high.'

GAME-FISHING PROFILES: YELLOWFIN TUNA

Yellowfin tuna are trans-oceanic migrants, passing through the Pemba Channel from August to October, providing fine sport for light-tackle enthusiasts, for in proportion to their size they are among the strongest of all game fish. Built for speed, they are distinguished from other tuna by their bright yellow finlets and belly. They often reach 1.5m (5ft) or more in length. Really big yellowfins can be exciting and exhausting to deal with.

Coral Garden and Razorback Reef: Superb site generally approached as drift dive but suitable for beginners as well as experts, depths from 16 to 30m (52–98ft). The 'garden', running north to south for a kilometre or more along Misali Island, consists of multitudinous corals, including fine gorgonian fans. Remarkable abundance of marine life from tiny reef fishes to giant groupers and great shoals of surgeon fish. Several large Napoleon wrasse live on the ridge. At its southernmost point the corals are not quite so resplendent though turtles are often found here. Razorback Reef and a further deep reef (experienced divers only) can be incorporated with this dive. Inside face of Razorback descends to around 30m (98ft), outer to about 40m (131ft). The deep reef can be approached from the top at 45m (148ft), from where sharks are occasionally seen.

Coral Mountain: Underwater mountain rising from a little over 80m (262ft) to around 18m (59ft), embellished by rose coral. Said to be suitable for novices as well as more advanced divers, despite the fact that 'at one point, hundreds of black snappers swirl around the diver'. Corals attract leaf fish and an abundance of blue-striped fusiliers. Larger fish, including rainbow runners, trevally and dog-tooth tuna hunt the area and manta rays (and in August the occasional thresher shark) sometimes cruise through. Octopuses and lobsters might be seen hiding among the crevices.

Makarere Reef: Interesting, undulating reef on sandy slope on southwestern edge of Misali. Series of coral knolls extends from top of reef at 8–10m (26–33ft) to sea bed at more than 30m (98ft). The corals provide shelter and sustenance for lobsters, moray eels, torpedo rays and many reef fish, while the sandy valleys are home to schools of surgeon- and unicornfish, roaming Napoleon wrasse and large spotted eagle rays. Dolphins (often spinners) frequent this site.

Mapinduzi: Arguably Misali's premier site, opposite Kijiji where channel enters bay. Corals not so prominent as on other sites though they include picturesque displays of green coral. Mapinduzi is a wall dive of moderate difficulty with depths from 15 to 45m (49–148ft). Eagle and manta rays, giant groupers, Napoleon wrasse, trevally and tunas, plus lots of giant triggers (which are said to be 'Pemban'...and [therefore] 'not aggressive').

Murray's Wall: Murray was apparently head of Maths at the Emirates International School in Dubai. Mapinduzi (named by Fundu Lagoon) means 'revolution' in Swahili. So now you know... Meanwhile this site on Utalimani Reef is a challenging wall consisting of four sites in one. Said to be a 'world-beater' in good visibility and 'a macro diver's heaven' in low visibility. Home to hundreds of jacks and sometimes a few sharks.

Above: *Perfect snorkelling and diving conditions.*

South Pemba

Emerald Reef/Serena's Folly: Named 'Emerald Reef' by Fundu Lagoon after the green coral that proliferates here, and 'Serena's Folly' by Swahili Divers for reasons best known to themselves and Serena, this is one of Pemba's most outstanding sites, off Pemba's southern tip by Panza Island. Despite its gentle, expansive slope from around 7–30m (23–98ft) and (normally) very good visibility, it usually has a current of at least 3 knots running, in one direction or the other, and is consequently for experienced divers only. Said to have 'every fish that Pemba has to offer'.

Mtangani and Mchengazi: Little way out from Shamiani Island off Pemba's southern coast. Experienced divers only. Characterized by steep wall. Said to be good for pelagics including sharks, barracuda, trevally and tuna. Depth around 30m (98ft).

Panza Wreck: Wreck (just southwest of Panza Island) of the Greek freighter *Paraportiani* that sank in 1969 between outer and inner reefs. She lies bows down in depths of 7–14m (23–46ft), large helm still in place. Due to fre-

Right: *A hawksbill turtle glides through the sea.*

quently strong currents this dive is best attempted at slack low or high tides by experienced divers only. Attracts a great diversity of marine life, including lots of glassfish as well as lionfish, juvenile Napoleon wrasse, trevally and a plethora of unicornfish. Invertebrates such as corals, crabs, nudibranches and sponges also common.

BIG-GAME (OFFSHORE SPORT) FISHING

The Zanzibar archipelago is noted as one of the best game fishing areas in the Indian Ocean but as with diving and snorkelling, this guide does not pretend to be an authority. Enthusiasts should therefore browse the Internet or contact the various big-game fishing companies in Zanzibar personally (a short list is provided in the 'At a Glance' section).

Boats vary but those owned by the better companies will be well designed, maintained and equipped, with more or less everything you might need, whether going out for the day or for sleepover trips. Tackle is provided though you can use your own, and skippers and crews are generally professional-minded experts, with a genuine (as well as vested) interest in your success and enjoyment.

A tag-and-release system is operated by some companies, whereby all fish, unless they are the first or the biggest to date that the individual has caught, or an East Africa/All Africa record, are returned to the water after being tagged.

THE BEST TIMES TO FISH

You can fish successfully around Zanzibar at all times of year though there are two main seasons. Traditionally when the northeast monsoon (*kaskazi*) is blowing, large numbers of billfish move into coastal waters to wreak havoc among the migrating shoals of yellowfin tuna. The yellowfin season runs from August to October inclusive, with the marlin and sailfish season close behind, from about mid-November to mid-March. Striped marlin are caught at this season, while large black or blue marlin are caught from September to December inclusive.

The Other Zanzibar at a Glance

Diving is possible throughout the year but the best time, especially in terms of visibility, is from about mid-October to mid-March. Whale sharks are most often seen between August and November and also in February, and humpback whales in September/October. Fishing is also possible at most times though the yellowfin season runs from August to October inclusive, with black or blue marlin from September through to December and striped marlin and sailfish from about mid-November to mid-March.

See chapters on Stone Town/Unguja/Pemba.

The various diving or fishing lodges and companies will provide boats to dive sites and fishing areas. Some people opt for 'live-aboard trips' (as opposed to basing yourself at one of the shore-side lodges or resorts). Such a trip allows you, for example, to circumnavigate Pemba in about five days, diving at various sites. Sadly Pemba Afloat, a live-aboard company once based in northwest Pemba, has now closed down and divers interested in such trips should

consult the Internet for future possibilities.

For accommodation and restaurant options, *see* the 'At a Glance' sections of previous chapters.

Diving/Fishing Companies
Stone Town
Bahari Divers, Forodhani St, tel: (0)748 254 786, www.zanzibar-diving.com
One Ocean – The Zanzibar Dive Centre, Kenyatta Rd, tel: (0)24 223 8374.

Nungwi/Kendwa
East African Diving and Water Sports, Jambo Brothers Bungalows, tel: (0)777 416 425/420 588.
FishingZanzibar.Com, Nungwi Village, tel: (0)756 442 203, email: info@ fishingzanzibar.com www.fishingzanzibar.com
Zanzibar Water Sports, Ras Nungwi Beach Hotel, tel: (0)24 223 3615, email: info@ zanzibarwatersports.com www.zanzibarwatersports.com Also at Paradise Beach Resort, Nungwi.
Sensation Divers, opposite Amaan Bungalows and at Nungwi Village Beach Resort, tel: (0)745 417 157, www.sensationdivers.com
Scuba Do, Kendwa, tel: (0)777 417 157, (0)748 415 179, www.scuba-do-zanzibar.com

Northeast Coast
One Ocean – The Zanzibar Dive Centre, Matemwe Beach Village, Matemwe, tel: (0)777 417 250; also at Blue Bay Beach Resort, Kiwengwa, tel: (0)24 224 0241, and Ocean Paradise Resort, Pwani/Mchangan), tel: (0)777 439 990, www.zanzibaroneocean.com
Zanzibar Beach Hotel Resort, Matemwe, tel: (0)777 417 782, www.zanzibar beachresort.com

Southeast Coast
Paje Dive Centre, Arabian Nights, Paje, tel: (0)24 224 0190/1, www.pajedive centre.com
Rising Sun Dive Centre, Breezes Beach Club, Dongwe, tel: (0)777 415 049, www.risingsun-zanzibar.com

Fumba Peninsula
Scuba Do, Fumba Beach Lodge, Fumba Peninsula, www.scuba-do-zanzibar.com

Pemba
Dive 710, Fundu Lagoon Resort, Wambaa Beach, tel: (0)24 223 2926, www.fundulagoon.com
One Earth Diving, Manta Reef Lodge, Ras Kigomasha, tel: (0)777 423 930, www.mantareeflodge.com
Swahili Divers, Kervan Saray, tel: (0)773 176 737/8 – let it ring out at least three times!)

Travel Tips

Tourist Information

There are many websites devoted to Zanzibar, easily accessed via a search engine such as Google. Typing in key words such as 'Zanzibar, beach hotels' or 'Zanzibar, diving', etc. will produce a host of responses.

Entry Requirements

Foreign nationals require a Tanzanian visa to enter Zanzibar and a passport valid for at least six months beyond the end of your intended stay. Single-entry three-month visas can be obtained from a Tanzanian embassy, high commission or consulate or on arrival at Tanzanian international airports or official border crossings. Keep a pen and some patience handy and be prepared to pass through Immigration twice, once on the mainland and again in Zanzibar.

Customs

Duty-free allowance in Tanzania is one litre of spirits, 200 cigarettes, 50 cigars or 250g of tobacco and 250ml of perfume. Personal effects don't usually elicit undue attention and passing through customs in Tanzania is generally much less stressful than it used to be, though if you are taking expensive presents you might be asked to pay duty. Tanzania is on a main drug route, however; don't be tempted to get involved in that particular can of worms.

Health Requirements

An up-to-date yellow fever certificate is all you should be required to produce.

Getting There

See 'Stone Town At a Glance'.
Airports: Dar es Salaam International Airport: tel: (0)22 284 2402; Zanzibar International Airport: tel: (0)24 223 0794.
Local Airlines: Coastal Aviation: tel: (0)24 223 3112; Precision Air: tel: (0)24 223 4520; ZanAir: tel: (0)24 223 3670.

What to Pack

Regarding clothing, light summery casuals are the norm, preferably cotton or cotton-rich, which are more comfortable in a tropical coastal climate. Shoes should also be casual and comfortable, with perhaps an old pair (or thick-soled trainers) for rock-pool rambling, in case you tread on sea urchins. Caps/hats are advisable and so are light woollens for early mornings and late evenings, which can be relatively cool, especially between June and October. Long sleeves are handy to help deter mosquitoes at dusk and also to roll down against possible sunburn.

If you are going on safari, which is probable, you might want to take clothes in neutral safari colours and light safari boots. Shirts should preferably have at least one pocket.

Take a good pair of binoculars if you intend to go on game drives, nature walks or birding trips, and a decent/very good camera, depending on your interest level. Most people now use digitals but you still need high mega-pixel bodies and good telephoto lenses (preferably image-stabilizing) if you want really good wildlife shots. Divers and snorkellers might want to take underwater cameras. Remember to take whatever storage cards and spare batteries you might need (you will probably take far more shots than you think) plus a portable battery charger. Laptops are useful for downloading photos or word-processing/Internet, etc. but they are an extra burden and like cameras and binoculars, easily stolen, so keep an eye on all attractive equipment.

If you intend to go camping or hiking a rucksack, Swiss army knife, reliable torch and water bottle/flask might be useful.

Experienced divers/snorkellers/fishing enthusiasts might want to take some of their own equipment, though all the best dive/fishing centres have quality equipment for hire.

Don't forget any medications/pharmacy products, etc. that you normally need or use, in appropriate quantities. Sunscreen is important to some people but seek medical advice if you have sensitive skin or skin-related allergies, and buy the appropriate grade.

Money Matters
Currency: Tanzania has a decimal currency based on the Tanzanian shilling. The more popular notes come in

---

PUBLIC HOLIDAYS

1 January • New Year's Day
12 January • Zanzibar Revolution Day
March/April • Good Friday and Easter Monday
7 April • Karume Day
26 April • Union Day
1 May • International Workers' Day
7 July • Saba Saba Day
8 August • Peasants' Day
14 October • Nyerere Day
9 December • Independence Day
25 December • Christmas

Holidays with variable dates:
Maulid • Celebrates birth of the Prophet Mohammed
Eid ul-Fitr • End of the Holy Month of Ramadan
Eid ul-Adga • Celebrates the sacrifice of Ismail and is the time for the main pilgrimage to Mecca.

---

denominations of 500, 2000, 5000 and 10,000 shillings, with coins of 100 and 200 shillings. Shopkeepers often have no small change and you are advised to carry a small amount of lower-value notes when shopping to avoid long delays (or the forfeit of your change).

Exchange: The American dollar has long been popular in Zanzibar and is even more so nowadays. Other hard currencies such as Pounds Sterling, euros, etc. are not so widely accepted (except of course in banks and bureaux de change). Credit cards are accepted at some of the more

up-market hotels, dive centres, etc. but don't rely on them. Travellers' cheques are more widely accepted but not always easy to cash and you will usually pay heavily for the privilege, as rates of exchange can be considerably less favourable compared with the mainland. It is probably best to balance pragmatism with security and take some hard cash (preferably US dollars), travellers' cheques and your credit card(s). In Pemba you should rely heavily on ready cash (preferably US dollars and Tanzanian shillings) and wherever you go in Tanzania make sure you have a supply of smaller denomination local bank notes, as waiting for change (if you ever get it) can be time-consuming.

Banks: Barclays Bank has a branch in Stone Town (tel: (0)24 223 7734) but otherwise banks in Zanzibar are national rather than international. Official opening hours are 08:30–15:00 Monday to Friday and 08:30–midday Saturday but be aware that some of them (especially the NMB in Chake Chake, the only place that deals in outgoing cash transactions in Pemba) can be frustratingly slow-moving. It is best, if possible, to conduct any banking transactions in Dar, Arusha, Nairobi, etc. before moving on to Zanzibar.

Accommodation
Hotels, resorts and guesthouses have mushroomed in Zanzibar (Unguja) in recent

years and come in all sizes and budget levels. Many represent good value for money, some don't. Hopefully this guide will point out some of the better ones but the choice of hotels is a very personal thing and you should do your own research, via the Internet or through your travel agent. Remember too that inconsistencies are often a way of life in places like Tanzania and that standards and rates can change quickly.

Transport

You can hire cars in Zanzibar though you need an internationally recognized licence (obtainable from motoring organizations before travelling to Zanzibar) or a national driving licence plus Zanzibar police permit. Either way you have to be authorized by a local police station. The great majority of visitors travel around by taxis or tourist minibuses, or by special shuttles organized by some of the larger resorts. Bicycles can be hired for more localized trips.

Travelling with a Local Travel Company

Most visitors to Zanzibar come as part of a pre-arranged package through a travel agent in their own country, but independent travellers might want to use a company based in Zanzibar. Some are listed under 'Stone Town at a Glance'.

Business Hours

Zanzibar has its own idiosyncratic timings. In places where traders are used to tourists, most shops will open between 09:00 and 10:00 and close between 17:00 and 18:00, though it's sometimes very hit-and-miss and some places will close for lunch (which can take up to two hours) or Friday prayers. During the holy month of Ramadan shops often stay closed until the evening.

Time Difference

Tanzanian/Zanzibar time is GMT + 3.

Communications

Tanzania's (and Zanzibar's) telephone and mobile phone facilities have improved over the past decade and Internet facilities are available in the larger towns and many of the more up-market hotels and resorts. Top-up cards for the various mobile phone companies (Celtel, Vodacom, etc.) are widely available. Tanzania's international tel code: 055; Dar es Salaam tel code: 022; Zanzibar tel code: 024; National Operator (English): 101; International Operator (English): 0101; Directory Enquiries and general queries: 135; Zanzibar Tourist Corporation: (0)24 223 2344.

Electricity

Standard power supplies are 220/240 volts accepting square three-pin plugs, so take the necessary adaptors. Power cuts are sometimes common in Tanzania but most of the better hotels/resorts have generators.

Weights and Measures

Tanzania uses the metric system.

Health Precautions

Possible recommended inoculations include yellow fever, tetanus, polio, hepatitis, meningitis and typhoid. The best course of action is to see a good doctor, explain exactly where you intend to go and for how long, and take his or her advice. Your doctor will also prescribe a course of anti-malarial tablets, etc. that

CONVERSION CHART		
FROM	**TO**	**MULTIPLY BY**
Millimetres	Inches	0.0394
Metres	Yards	1.0936
Metres	Feet	3.281
Kilometres	Miles	0.6214
Square kilometres	Square miles	0.386
Hectares	Acres	2.471
Litres	Pints	1.760
Kilograms	Pounds	2.205
Tonnes	Tons	0.984

To convert Celsius to Fahrenheit: x 9 ÷ 5 + 32

USEFUL PHRASES

ENGLISH	SWAHILI
Hello	Jambo
How are you?	Habari?
Fine/OK	Mzuri
Thank you	Asante
(very much)	(sana)
Welcome!	Karibu!
	(pl. Karibuni)
Excuse me	Samahani
Goodbye	Kwaheri
Yes	Ndiyo
No	Hapana
Today	Leo
Tomorrow	Kesho
Hot	Moto
Cold	Baridi
Hotel	Hoteli
Room	Chumba
Bed	Kitanda
Shop	Duka
One	Moja
Two	Mbili
Three	Tatu
Four	Ine
Five	Tano

you should continue to follow for a short period (again your doctor should advise you) after your return. Should you fall sick soon after returning you must inform your doctor that you have recently been in a tropical/malarial area.

AIDS is widespread in Tanzania and Zanzibar now has its problems, thanks in part to increased tourism. The options and dangers are well known and avoidable, but be aware that alcohol and drugs, and the relaxed, friendly conditions that prevail in Zanzibar, can increase vulnerability.

Water should not be drunk directly from the tap, even in the best hotels, or used for brushing teeth, etc. Most hotels and resorts provide guests with mineral water or water that has been boiled and filtered, and reasonably cheap mineral water is available throughout Zanzibar, from various stores and dukas (small shops).

Health Services

Health care in Tanzania and Zanzibar leaves a lot to be desired, though in the major cities such as Dar es Salaam there are good doctors and reasonable hospitals. Risks of serious illness or accidents are minimal but in the end you opt to take them or you don't.

Hospitals and Clinics (Unguja): Afya Medical Centre: tel: (0)24 223 1228; Mnazi Mmoja Hospital: tel: (0)24 223 1071/2/3; Zanzibar Medical Group: tel: (0)24 223 1424.

Security

Until recently Zanzibar was one of the safest places on earth and probably still is. However, thieving and mugging have increased. Don't let this stop you from relaxing but be aware that such things sometimes occur. Check with your hotel/resort before embarking on long walks, especially alone and/or along lonely beaches, and if you do set off, do not carry expensive items or attractive-looking bags. And of course, don't go walking too far at night.

In the event of an attempted mugging it is advisable not to resist. The mugger(s) will then almost certainly make off without physically harming you.

Drugs are a growing problem and Stone Town in particular has its minority of serious addicts, some of whom can be particularly annoying as they often pose as would-be guides. Very few are physically aggressive and most will leave you alone after a few minutes. Decline any advances firmly but politely.

'Beach boys' in certain resorts can also be a nuisance, particularly to young women, but politely ignoring or declining their advances (normally no more than cheekily exploratory banter) is the best answer.

In the case of fairly serious or serious theft, muggings, etc., consult your hotel/resort people and go with one of them to report the incident to the nearest police station. Don't expect to get your things back (though this sometimes happens) but at least it might help to focus attention on the problems in that area; the authorities are sensitive to negative issues of this kind.

Would-be tourists concerned about Zanzibar's Islamic nature in these days of heightened religious tensions should be reassured. Zanzibar is still a peaceful, tolerant place and there are few, if any, recorded cases of tourists being seriously threatened or harmed due to religious bigotry. On the contrary, the great majority of Zanzibaris are welcoming and easy-going, though of course they and their beliefs should be

GOOD READING

Non-fiction (General)
l-Maamiry, *Omani Sultans in Zanzibar* (Lancers Books)
Lyne, Robert, *Zanzibar in Contemporary Times* (Gallery)
Mercer, Graham, *Bagamoyo, Town of Palms* (G Mercer)
Patience, Kevin, *Zanzibar: Slavery and the Royal Navy* (K Patience)
Pitcher, Gemma and Jafferji, Javed, *Magic of Zanzibar* (Gallery)
Reute, Emily, *Memoirs of an Arabian Princess* (Gallery)
Sherrif, Prof. Abdul, *Historical Zanzibar* (Gallery)
Unwin, Sheila, *The Arab Chest* (Arabian Publishing)

Non-fiction (Field Guides)
Lieske, E and Myers, R, *Coral Reef Fishes* (Princeton University Press)

Richmond, MD (ed), *Field Guide to the Seashores of East Africa* (SIDA/University of Dar es Salaam)
Stevenson, T and Fanshawe, J, *Field Guide to the Birds of East Africa* (Poyser)

Non-fiction (Exploration)
Bierman, John, *Dark Safari: The Life Behind the Legend of Henry Morton Stanley* (Sceptre)
Dugard, Martin, *Into Africa: The Adventures of Stanley and Livingstone* (Bantam)

Fiction
Foden, Giles, *Zanzibar* (Faber & Faber)
Gurnah, Abdulrazak, *By the Sea* (Bloomsbury Publishing)
Gurnah, Abdulrazak, *Paradise* (New Press)

---

respected, especially during the holy month of Ramadan, when Muslims fast during daylight hours. Tourists in Zanzibar at this time should avoid eating or drinking in public (except of course in their hotels and resorts, or in restaurants).

Political violence, however, is not unknown in the Isles, and although it rarely, if ever, affects tourists directly, it would be wise to avoid Zanzibar during national elections, in the immediate run-up to them or in their immediate aftermath.

Emergencies
Ambulance/Fire/Police (respectively, but don't expect too much!) : 112/111/999.

Etiquette
Zanzibaris are extremely tolerant, easy-going people on the whole but please be sensitive towards their (mainly Islamic) culture, which rates modesty, especially among women, very highly. Do not wear revealing clothes away from the beach. Similarly, kissing and petting in public can be offensive, as can drunkenness or other anti-social behaviour.

Do not photograph people, especially Zanzibari women, without their permission, or take photographs, anywhere in Tanzania, of military installations, police posts, bridges, etc. If you or your driver are stopped and questioned by

police be courteous and preferably good-humoured, no matter how irritated you feel, but don't just shell out *chai* money (bribes) either, especially if you have done nothing wrong. Tourists are not usually bothered by police for more than a few minutes.

If you are in Zanzibar during the holy month of Ramadan, when Muslims fast during daylight hours, it is good manners not to eat or drink openly in public (outside hotels/resorts). Most Muslims find fasting a privilege and are very tolerant towards non-Muslims, but they also appreciate your respect.

Finding Your Way
Walking is undoubtedly the best (and often only) way to negotiate the fascinating narrow streets of Stone Town.

Guides are not essential, but the best of them, often older, know their town. Visitors should ask for a guide at their hotel or any tourist centre.

If you choose to discover Stone Town on your own, however, you can lose yourself in the maze of alleyways without too much fear of being lost for long, or of having anything stolen, though visitors should use a little common sense (e.g. by not wearing expensive jewellery).

Please respect Islamic modesty by wearing clothes that are not too revealing.

Language
The national language of Tanzania is Swahili, said to be at its purest in Zanzibar.

INDEX

Page numbers in **bold** indicate pictures.